Horoscope 2022

Unlocking Astrological Forecasts for the 12 Zodiac Signs Using Birth Charts and Planet Positions

Your Free Gift (only available for a limited time)

Thanks for getting this book! If you want to learn more about various spirituality topics, then join Mari Silva's community and get a free guided meditation MP3 for awakening your third eye. This guided meditation mp3 is designed to open and strengthen ones third eye so you can experience a higher state of consciousness. Simply visit the link below the image to get started.

https://spiritualityspot.com/meditation

Contents

Introduction

Over the last few years, the whole world has faced innumerable challenges, but now we find ourselves – yet again – in a new year. As is always the case, the big question on everyone's minds is what this year might bring. Seeking to answer this question, one might look toward astrological forecasts for the year ahead. Whether you are new to astrology or are already a seasoned astrology enthusiast, this book will provide you with an informative, easily digestible, and comprehensive overview to help you toward that end. Through a combination of accessibility and useful information, this book will bring astrology closer to even a beginner while leaving nothing out. This means that you'll get a detailed look at what 2022 has in store for you without the associated confusion that often accompanies such overviews.

Apart from an overview of the new year and what it has in store for your sign, this book will also provide insight into important astrological events that are coming in 2022. It contains instructions and advice about what we can expect from 2022. These are only some of the ways you'll find this book stands out and, by the end, you should have a thorough understanding of what astrology has in store for you and what you can do to nudge the odds even more in your favor.

Astrology is a sophisticated system with many layers and a lot of depth, and it's much more than just an easy way to pass the time while reading the morning paper. It warrants further study because of the interesting things it can tell us, but it's also worth remembering that some of the most prominent human civilizations in the past have held astrology in high regard. These civilizations include the ancient Greeks and Babylonians, who developed much of the early astrological system, and ancient Romans and Arabs, who preserved the knowledge and improved upon it.

Over time, we have come even further in our understanding of astrology and its meaning in our lives. We also know much more than ever about the celestial bodies that adorn our skies and affect our lives. It only takes a moderate amount of reading, even for the most inexperienced beginner, to grasp the fundamentals of this knowledge and harness the insights of astrology for their own benefit.

Chapter 1: Overview of 2022

Between the ongoing pandemic and other issues facing the world today, it's no secret that many people have had a rough couple of years. As always, however, there are many reasons to be optimistic, which will certainly hold true for 2022. When it comes to predicting what might lie ahead of us, astrology is always there to lend a helping hand and give us some useful hints. Of course, astrology isn't an exact science or a fortune-telling crystal ball, and the predictions it gives us aren't absolute truths and should not be taken as such. However, the planets, stars, and other celestial bodies in our skies will be positioned in a certain way; it's up to astrological interpretation as to what that positioning might imply.

The world itself has seen better days, so the big question on most people's minds is how 2022 might be different and whether we can expect things to get worse, better, or stay largely the same. One of the biggest hopes for the new year is that the ongoing COVID-19 pandemic will die down so that life might return to some semblance of normalcy for billions of people around the world. When this happens is currently a point of debate, and nobody can know for certain. There are, however, reasons to be optimistic, such as the continuously growing prevalence of vaccination.

The eventual dying down of the pandemic will bring with it several other optimistic outcomes as well. The economic uncertainty accompanying the outbreak should also subside with the pandemic, alleviating some of the stress. This will largely result from the gradual removal of various restrictions that have been keeping a stranglehold over economic activity worldwide, not just in America. Socially and politically, the future is always difficult to predict, but in the worst-case scenario, things will stay the same as they were in 2021. With the potential weakening of the pandemic, we can also hope for more stability and less tension, but the potential for great change is always present.

Like any other new year, in 2022, you can count on having ample opportunities to make positive changes and good decisions, adopt new mindsets, and improve your life. Freedom and control - the kind that comes from deep within you - are something that can't be taken away from you, but they are also something you have to reach out for and grasp. Astrology will help you get a general idea of what you can expect and how you can better spot such opportunities, but it will ultimately be up to you to use the lemons life gives you.

There are astrological indications that 2022 will be a year of changes worldwide, bringing opportunities for us to reevaluate our paths and mend some of the problems, divisions, and misunderstandings that have accumulated. Global processes are driven by billions of individuals, though, which is why everyone needs to start with themselves. Embrace the opportunities the new year will bring you, try your best to do good for yourself and those around you, and you'll have done your part.

General Astrological Forecast

The '20s seem to be a time for changes, and it appears that 2022 will undoubtedly play its part in that process. Numerous astrological events will have an important effect on this year; in one of the later chapters, we'll look at the most important among those events in more detail. One of these upcoming astrological events is the long-awaited return of Pluto in February. While official astronomy has stopped considering Pluto a planet a while ago, this celestial body continues to play an important astrological role in our lives. Because of its distance from the sun, Pluto orbits around the sun in a very wide circle, making its revolution around our star a very long journey. Pluto hasn't finished one such journey since exactly 1776, the year of America's declaration of independence.

The finalization of Pluto's revolution, which will happen in the sign of Capricorn, might bring significant ramifications in the grand scheme of things. Because Pluto tends to motivate change while also providing a doorway for the forces of both creation and destruction, a great number of people might find themselves feeling like letting go of certain things. How this might translate into worldly events remains to be seen, but Pluto's governance over power in all its forms, including human power over others, might spell significant changes.

Jupiter and Neptune will also be major influences in 2022. Jupiter will bring its imposing, expansive presence into the picture while Neptune fosters human intuition and touch with the mystical and unknown. The master of all that's underneath, especially in the minds and hearts of people, Neptune has the potential to bring out a lot of good things in people this year. The strong influence of these two planets in 2022 is likely to provide favorable conditions for various human endeavors in the fields of art, technology, and invention. In that light, societies worldwide will continue to explore their own nature in an attempt to better understand the position and prospects of humanity in a world increasingly dominated by technology.

For fire signs, Aries, Leo, and Sagittarius, desirable influences in 2022 will come primarily from Mars, Jupiter, and the asteroid Chiron. Mars' entrance into Sagittarius early in January will provide for an epic confluence of intense forces, bringing the intensity that Sagittarius craves. Such conditions provide the best opportunity for adventure, Sagittarius's middle name. Jupiter will also spend considerable time in Aries in the second half of the year. At the same time, the sign will also rub shoulders with Chiron. Aries will certainly not lack strength and perseverance in 2022.

As is the nature of earth signs, Taurus, Virgo, and Capricorn will use their logic and their reasoning abilities to navigate their way through 2022 as successfully as they can. Uranus should bring even greater reserves of patience and calm to Taurus, adding to the sign's naturally restrained and controlled demeanor. This stability will ensure that Taurus can withstand all challenges, should they arise in 2022. The aforementioned entrance of Pluto into Capricorn will make people under this sign even more reflective and introspective than usual, making 2022 a good year for soul-searching.

All three air signs, including Libra, Aquarius, and Gemini, will experience lunar influence as the moon enters the signs in mid-April, early August, and early December. These already highly dynamic, restless, even fickle signs will be prone to distraction as the moon passes. Still, these distractions will be nothing that the adaptable air signs can't handle.

The water signs, including Cancer, Scorpio, and Pisces, will be influenced by astrological events and positions of Neptune and Jupiter above all. Neptune, the modern ruler of Pisces, will spend a lot of time in the sign, making the intuition that Pisces is famous for as strong as ever. However, Neptune will eventually go retrograde in June, which can be of some concern for Pisces.

We will go into more detail about retrogrades and other astrological events and what they mean. Still, suffice it to say that they can cause issues and that 2022 will have plenty of them. The retrogrades of various planets in 2022 will bring things like waning of the qualities and strengths of some of the signs in a given period, personal drama, some instability, and other challenges. Challenges are there to be overcome and make us stronger in the process. Hence, retrogrades aren't necessarily something to get worried about or discouraged by. In fact, it can sometimes be quite the opposite, as a bit of adversity can also be a force of creation in our lives.

Mercury will be the absolute king of retrogrades this year, going through four of them in total. The planet god of communication will retrograde through Aquarius, Gemini, Libra, and Capricorn, stirring things up all year and even a couple of weeks into 2023. These retrogrades are expected to affect life's social aspects, communication, and intellectual pursuits. You might end up reevaluating some of your relationships, which won't necessarily be a bad thing. Still, you must keep in mind that the planet that affects communication won't be at the top of its game in 2022.

In general, it's important to remember that each challenge is an opportunity to learn and grow as a person. The influence of expansive Jupiter will be especially important in that regard. If you run into turbulence at any point in 2022, you should use it as a hint that some aspects of your life might need to be reevaluated. Being a time for a change, 2022 will present you with opportunities to change your bad habits, but it might also reveal that it's not always you that's the problem. Indeed, toxic relationships are something you must become aware of before you solve the problem, and 2022 might be just the year for that.

Chinese Astrology

Before we get on with the rest of our themes of Western astrology, let's take a little detour and take a look toward the Far East. For example, China is a civilization that has had a deep interest in the stars for thousands of years, spawning an intricate system of astrology that differs in many ways from what we are familiar with in the West. The goals of Chinese astrology are largely the same, and the readings seek answers mostly from the same objects that we all see in the sky. However, the methodological and systemic side of things is where some interesting differences lie.

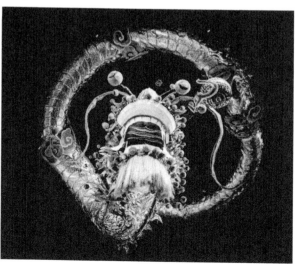

The height of early Chinese astronomy and astrology came during the Han dynasty, which ruled for centuries after 202 BCE, although the origins of Chinese astrology go further back. The Chinese zodiac is certainly one of the oldest in the world and has been used as a horoscope system for about as long. Just like the zodiac we know, the Chinese one is divided into twelve signs, all of which are represented by their respective animals that, in turn, represent years. Since every animal on the Chinese zodiac has its years, a person's birth year determines their sign. The Chinese zodiac animals include the Rat, Ox, Tiger, Rabbit, Dragon, Snake, Horse, Sheep, Monkey, Rooster, Dog, and Pig.

Chinese astrology also has natural elements like Western astrology, except those five elements are somewhat different. These elements are water, wood, fire, earth, and metal, whereas, in Western astrology, there are fire, air, earth, and water. Just like in the West, Chinese astrology takes into account the positions of planets, the sun, and the moon at the time of an individual's birth as a way of determining what might lie ahead in their life. Chinese astrology tries to predict the kind of attitude and potential a person might have based on these astrological indicators. Each animal in the Chinese zodiac is also associated with certain traits and behaviors.

According to Chinese astrology, 2022 will be a year of the Tiger, beginning with February 1 and ending on January 21, 2023. The last few years of the Tiger were in 2010, 1998, 1986, 1974, 1962, 1950, and 1938. Like in 2022, Chinese astrology had certain predictions for all those previous years of the Tiger, based on the sign's inherent implications. In general, in Chinese astrology and culture, the Tiger is symbolic of all those things that we associate with lions in the West. It is a sign that exhibits strength, boldness, and courage. The Tiger is also thought to banish evil and misfortune, which is why this animal's symbol is a popular good luck charm.

All of this spells quite a few interesting predictions that Chinese astrology has for the year ahead of us, which is the year of the Water-

Tiger. While the Tiger will be the ruling animal throughout the year, elemental water will act as the main energy source. The predictions imply that the year will be intense, which might be a very good thing for most. There is a lot of determinism in what Chinese astrology forecasts for 2022, but there are also strong hints that the year will be one of novelty and spontaneous experiences. A degree of adversity might come because of all this, but this natural trade-off will be nature's way of strengthening us.

Just like Western astrology, the Chinese horoscope for 2022 predicts a time of drastic changes and numerous surprises, for better or worse. All twelve Chinese signs will be well-advised to look out for opportunities in these tumultuous times, which might be plentiful and might come disguised as hardships. A year of that much novelty and unknown territory will necessitate action, preparedness, and an awareness of one's goals and desires. These stormy conditions will also make it easier to let go of troublesome pasts and focus on new endeavors.

The energy that elemental water will bring into the year will be one of temperance. This influence will offset some of the more intense energies associated with the Tiger and some of 2022's influential planets. In relationships, for instance, this might foreshadow a degree of cooling of passions and intensity, but this just means there will be more room for other aspects of intimate human communication. With the blinding effects of intense passion somewhat curtailed, there will be more opportunity for meaningful conversations, objective analysis, and depth. As a result, solid relationships can only get stronger and more meaningful while toxic, dysfunctional ones will be exposed for what they are, helping you let go more easily. This is yet another overlap between Western and Chinese astrology forecasts for 2022, which will undoubtedly be the year of reevaluation when it comes to relationships.

It also appears that the new Chinese year will bring a strengthening of willpower and a heightened ability to think objectively in general, not just in relationships. It will be the year to stop, think, analyze, and arrive at logical conclusions instead of reacting emotionally and irrationally. This is further illustrated by the fact that the Water Tiger is the most rational and least careless of the five elemental variations of the sign. In this context, methodical, critical thinking doesn't necessarily mean slower thinking – quite the contrary. The Water Tiger can think and be careful while still maintaining a quick wit.

On the global scale, Chinese astrological readings hint at the continued distrust that citizens worldwide feel toward their governments. The ongoing pandemic has greatly exacerbated this problem and accompanying epidemiological prevention measures. Given the energy the Tiger brings into the year, the distrust might become even more intense. However, restraint and reason should prevail thanks to the mitigating effects of elemental water. Just as 2022 brings opportunities to reevaluate and mend relationships on a personal level, the same might follow in politics throughout the world.

All told, the Chinese horoscope for 2022 predicts a productive, dynamic, and progressive year full of opportunities, transitions, and changes. As accurate as these predictions might be, it's always going to be up to us to act on the presented opportunities and enact positive changes where possible. The Water Tiger's energy might provide the fuel and the steam, but it's ultimately us who have to steer the ship. Chinese astrology often arrives at similar predictions as Western astrology does, but it provides a unique perspective and additional cultural context to reading stars. As such, you might find enrichment in studying Chinese astrology in a bit more depth, at least to the extent of learning what your sign is and what it means for you.

Chapter 2: The 12 Zodiac Signs

Before we proceed to a more detailed overview of what 2022 has in store for each sign and in terms of important astrological events, this chapter will go over the twelve zodiac signs and what makes them special when compared to each other. Understanding each sign's nature, personality, and astrological properties is the first and most crucial step to understanding how to read what astrology has to tell you.

While people's sun signs tend to get the most attention and are usually discussed in horoscopes and regular astrology, each person actually has two additional signs. There are moon signs and rising (ascendant) signs, apart from sun signs. The moon sign corresponds to the zodiac sign in which the moon was at the time of your birth, while the ascendant sign is the one that just begins to appear on the horizon as you are born. All three of these signs are important aspects of your birth chart and are taken into account in detailed birth chart readings. Still, we will focus primarily on your sun sign for much of our annual forecast.

Aries – The Ram

- **Date Range:** March 21 – April 19

- **Birthstone:** Bloodstone

- **Lucky Day:** Tuesday, Saturday, Friday

- **Power Color:** Red

- **Lucky Number:** 1, 6, 8, 9, 17

The Aries symbol is the Ram, which is the constellation that this sign has been associated with since antiquity. The Ram had a prominent place in Babylonian astrology and was revered as an important influencer of agriculture and shepherds. The constellation and its symbolic importance were also notable in ancient Egypt, where the Ram was mostly associated with Amun-Ra, one of the most important Egyptian deities. In Egyptian religion, this god was associated with fertility, creativity, and the beginning of spring. The Ram's symbolism in Greek mythology was embodied by Chrysomallos, the winged ram adorned with the Golden Fleece and the rescuer of Phrixus and Helle, the children of mythological king Athamas. The sign's name is also derived from the Greek god of war, Ares.

The sign's date range is between March 21 and April 19. Aries' element is fire, and just like the sign's first position among the zodiac signs, the element certainly goes hand in hand with the Ram's personality. That fire element is what feeds the Ram's impulsive, assertive, and headstrong personality. Aries is also the first of the four signs with a cardinal quality, all of which mark the beginning of one of the four seasons, making them natural initiators and leaders. This trait is especially pronounced in the Ram, who heralds the beginning of spring.

The dominant ruling planet in Aries is Mars, which is the influence responsible for Aries' frequent fearlessness and even combativeness. The sun is exalted in this sign, and those born with the sun in Aries are known for their copious reserves of energy and confidence. On the other hand, Venus is in detriment when in Aries, which is the opposite of its preferred home in Libra, diminishing its influences of connectivity and peaceful disposition that struggle against the confronting nature of Aries. Similarly, Saturn is in fall when in Aries, which usually manifests in restlessness and impulsiveness, the opposite of the qualities Saturn has in Libra.

As a moon sign, Aries can be hotheaded, but their familiarity with their own needs and desires brings a degree of stability. An ascendant Aries is a natural, strong initiator who will often go head-first into the unknown and ask questions later, relying on their instincts above all else. This nature is something that Rams should follow in 2022, as their initiative and boldness are likely to be rewarded financially when Venus enters the sign in May. Bold moves in the Ram's love life and career are also likely to yield results thanks to the entrance of Jupiter.

Taurus – The Bull

- **Date Range:** April 20 – May 20
- **Birthstone:** Sapphire
- **Lucky Day:** Monday, Friday, Saturday
- **Power Color:** Green, pink
- **Lucky Number:** 5, 6, 9, 12

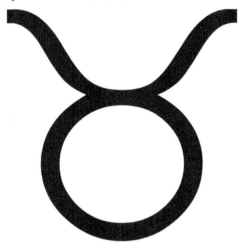

The symbol of Taurus is the Bull, and its constellation has held significance for people looking toward the stars since the early Bronze Age. Back in the day, the constellation's position in the Northern Hemisphere was used to determine the spring equinox and, like numerous other signs, Taurus was important for agriculture and related worship across various ancient civilizations. In Greek mythology, Taurus is also a symbol of the White Bull, which was a form taken by Zeus to court Europa. Zeus was said to have taken the princess on his back across the Mediterranean to Crete in this form. Minos was conceived and became the king of Crete and the subject of many Greek myths.

Taurus has a fixed quality, being the first of four such signs of the zodiac, all of which occupy the central period of the seasons. Among these stable and enduring signs, Taurus occupies the middle of spring, which provides the Bull with the stability and strength that the sign is renowned for. Taureans like to have strong roots and to keep their feet firmly on the ground. Their stability and endurance often translate to stubbornness and, once the Bull has made up his mind, they can become virtually immovable. The sign's earth element is the heaviest and most solid of the elements, further strengthening the Bull's virtues of patience, dependability, and perseverance.

Taurus is ruled by Venus, which finds a nocturnal home in the sign. Taurus' nature allows Venus to shine in all its main qualities like affection, artistry, and love of pleasure. Folks born with Venus in Taurus tend to be creative, patient, dedicated, friendly, and have a strong taste for the finer things in life. On the other hand, the warlike energy of Mars is at odds with Taurus' nature, putting the planet to detriment when in this sign.

As with other signs, the moon and ascendant Taureans tend to acquire even more shades and depths of the sign's inherent nature. Taureans will benefit from exercising their inherent patience as 2022 goes underway because of retrograde Venus early in the year. In time, however, things will start looking quite up after the eclipses and conjunctions that are scheduled throughout the year. Ford Taurus, 2022 will be the year to evolve as a person.

Gemini – The Twins

- **Date Range**: May 21 – June 20

- **Birthstone:** Agate

- **Lucky Day:** Monday, Wednesday, Thursday

- **Power Color**: Yellow, light green

- **Lucky Number:** 5, 7, 14, 23

The symbol of Gemini, which is the Twins, comes from Greek mythology and the story of Castor and Pollux, the legendary sons of Leda. She was another mythological princess whom Zeus had seduced in one of his animal forms, this time that of a swan. As the story goes, the conception of this relationship resulted in Leda laying two eggs from which the brothers hatched. Like the Greeks before them, the ancient Romans continued preserving and developing the myth of Castor and Pollux, portraying them as legendary horsemen. According to the myth, the brothers found rest in the heavens after their time on earth as the Gemini constellation.

Gemini's element is air, characterized by its lightness, formlessness, and the ease with which it disperses over the world. The air element is part of what's behind Gemini's apparent ability to be "all over the place." They are folks who like to be on the move, gather knowledge, establish new contacts, and explore the world to satisfy their intense curiosity. As such, Geminis are even prone to mischief and getting themselves into trouble, which is exacerbated by their mutable quality. The first of the four mutable signs, Gemini is adaptable and finds itself situated right at the transition of two seasons, hence the sign's frequent restlessness.

Like Virgo, Gemini is ruled by Mercury and is its daytime (diurnal) home. Gemini's adaptability works well with the fluid, curious, and analytical energy brought forth by Mercury. Folks born with Mercury in Gemini tend to be shrewd, quick-thinking, communicative, adaptable, and, above all, curious. However, Jupiter's entrance into the sign is detrimental as Gemini's nature clashes with Jupiter's orientation toward the big picture.

The expressive, curious, and outgoing Gemini's traits can be quite pronounced when talking about the moon sign. In extreme cases, moon Geminis can begin to enjoy the attention a bit too much, so they need to keep this in check. Ascendant Geminis are largely the same and, like many Geminis, can become so restless and dynamic that it begins to hurt their relationships. 2022 will be a year of numerous retrogrades for Mercury, but Geminis will still have things to look forward to, especially in summer and when the asteroid Ceres enters the sign.

Cancer – The Crab

- **Date Range:** June 21 – July 22
- **Birthstone**: Emerald
- **Lucky Day**: Tuesday, Friday, Thursday, Sunday
- **Power Color**: Violet, white
- **Lucky Number:** 2, 3, 15, 20

Cancer's recognizable symbol is the crab, which is similar to many of the other shelled and armored creatures that the constellation has been identified within the mythologies of the past. The associated animal was the scarab beetle in ancient Egypt, also known as the sacred scarab. This dung beetle was considered a symbol of immortality, and its reverence in ancient Egyptian society is evident by the scarab-shaped amulets left behind as artifacts. Babylonians had similar ideas about the constellation, associating it with a god in charge of guiding the deceased through the underworld. In ancient Greece, the Crab was associated with Karkinos, a mythological crab in service of goddess Hera and an enemy of Hercules.

Cancer is the second cardinal sign and, as such, retains this quality's traits that revolve around initiative and leadership as it heralds the beginning of summer. This season's abundance of sunlight and solar energy is of utmost importance for the Crab and some of its more intense traits such as authority and care. The sign's water element retains the fluidity and adaptability of air, but thanks to its weight and tangibility, it provides the Crab with a degree of stability and calmness that some air signs might lack.

The Crab is ruled by the moon, seen in many ancient civilizations as a protector of our world and a guide that lights our path in the night. Just like the sign's ruler, a Cancer has the potential to be the protector, nurturer, and guide to their loved ones. A Cancer truly shines when Jupiter enters the sign at birth. Jupiter's exaltation in Cancer further intensifies the Crab's benevolence, strength, and authority. Saturn will be detrimental if it enters this sign, with the ability to make some Cancers overly protective and unwilling to express their emotions.

In 2022, the emotionally sophisticated and nurturing Cancer would be well advised to make sure they aren't neglecting themselves while caring for others too much. The second half of the year is likely to bring plenty of good fortune into the lives of Cancers, especially in the realms of finance and romance.

Leo – The Lion

- **Date Range:** July 23 – August 22
- **Birthstone:** Onyx
- **Lucky Day:** Tuesday, Friday, Sunday
- **Power Color:** Gold, yellow, orange
- **Lucky Number:** 1, 3, 10, 19

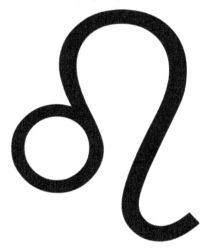

The lion symbolizes the fifth sign of the zodiac, the constellation associated with the sign since antiquity. As always, Greek mythology has played a major part in shaping the symbolism of this sign, particularly through the story of Hercules overcoming a legendary Lion. Such stories are most likely the origin of various associations we make with lions in astrology and popular culture, including courage, heroism, and triumph.

Leos garner their strength, stability, and perseverance from their fixed quality, being the second of the four fixed zodiac signs. In the middle of summer, Lion's traits are especially intense in this regard. Leos tend to be confident, self-assured, stable, and they usually enjoy being the center of attention. The sign's fire element also contributes to these traits, akin to how Lion can shine and assert himself among other people and in anything they do.

Expectedly, Leo is ruled by the sun, and, just like Cancer and the moon, Leo and the sun have an exclusive relationship. The sign of Leo allows the sun to fully realize its imposing, dominant force that reigns supreme over all of nature. Just as the sun is the celestial body around which the rest of our solar system revolves, the Lion often finds himself as the center and pillar of teams, communities, families, and other collectives. Saturn is the planet that's in detriment in this sign since its energy of discipline, boundaries, and judgment is at odds with Leo's prideful and forceful nature.

2022 is poised to be a very good year for Leo, thanks to the sign's special relationship with the sun. The only problem for Leo can be the two solar eclipses that are scheduled to occur during the year, which can lead to some instability in Leo's life. These turbulences will take on more of a transformative role as the Lion will eventually come out on top, stronger than before.

Virgo – The Maiden

- **Date Range**: August 23 – September 22
- **Birthstone:** Carnelian
- **Lucky Day:** Monday, Wednesday, Thursday
- **Power Color:** Silver, beige
- **Lucky Number:** 5, 14, 15, 23, 32

The Babylonians were probably the first civilization to give importance to the Virgo constellation by associating it with Shala, an important goddess of grain and wife to Adad, the Mesopotamian god of weather. Similarly, Greek mythology viewed Virgo as the goddess Demeter, strongly associated with the abundance of earth and agriculture. Roman mythology continued to maintain and develop the agricultural association as well.

Virgo is the second mutable sign, to which it owes the ability to adapt and change. It occupies a position at the end of summer, characterized by diminishing sunlight and warmth, subtly and gradually giving way to the onset of autumn. This change is most apparent in the ever-shortening daylight, which is an important influence on Virgo. Unlike the sign's mutable quality, its earth element provides a solid and stable counterbalance.

Unlike Gemini, Virgo is yet another sign ruled by Mercury, representing the planet's nocturnal home. This allows the planet's influences to manifest through qualities such as communication, good judgment, analytical abilities, and physical dexterity. In general, folks born with Mercury in Virgo are known to be perceptive and clever. Detrimental effects can occur when Jupiter enters the sign at birth because it tends to be at odds with Virgo's need for detailed organization, efficiency, and stability. A Virgo with this placement might end up trying too hard to compensate for Jupiter's detriment, such as by focusing too much on fine details and missing the bigger picture.

In 2022, Virgos will be tempted to completely disregard their own needs by focusing too hard on helping other people. This natural inclination, coupled with the fickle behavior of Mercury in 2022, means that Virgos should exercise caution in this regard and make sure that they take care of themselves before (and in addition to) others. Nonetheless, the year will likely bring positive surprises, especially on the love front and around your birthday.

Libra – The Scales

- **Date Range:** September 23 – October 22
- **Birthstone:** Peridot
- **Lucky Day:** Sunday, Monday, Tuesday
- **Power Color:** Blue, green
- **Lucky Number:** 4, 6, 13, 15, 24

Libra's symbol, the Scales, was in antiquity, associated with justice and law, just as it is today. This association stems from its ancient connection with the Greek goddess Themis, who was in charge of justice. The Greeks believed Themis to be the daughter of Uranus and Gaia. Like most other Greek myths, the myth of Themis and the Scales of justice continued in ancient Rome and was also associated with Venus and Aphrodite. Eventually, Themis found rest in the heavens as a constellation.

As the third cardinal sign of the zodiac, Libra finds itself situated at the beginning of autumn in the Northern Hemisphere. The diminishing of light and heat after the autumn equinox makes for a season of slowing down and of reduced intensity, which translates to Libra. Like the autumn equinox holds an equal amount of light and dark, Libra strives for balance in everything they do. A concern for justice and equality is common for folks born under this sign. Libra's air element contributes to the sign's easygoing, dynamic nature.

Libra is ruled by Venus, which finds in this sign the daytime home, as opposed to Taurus. Libra's harmonious and balanced nature allows Venus to fully exert its energy of peace, diplomacy, and love. With Venus in Libra, people are likely to be graceful, elegant, soft-spoken, diplomatic, and highly capable in social situations. Furthermore, Saturn is exalted in the sign of Libra, combining its inclination toward discipline and keen perception with Libra's sense of justice. With this placement, you are likely to end up as a highly measured and perceptive person with good judgment and a strong sense of what's right. However, the confrontational and warlike properties of Mars will certainly be detrimental if the planet enters this sign at birth.

Because Venus will be in retrograde in early 2022, the year might start a bit slow for Libra. Rather than being a period of diminished love and warmth that you can otherwise count on from Venus, this period can be perceived as an opportunity to plan, reorganize, and get ready for the rest of the year, bringing many great opportunities in the realm of relationships and finances.

Scorpio – The Scorpion

- **Date Range:** October 23 – November 21
- **Birthstone:** Topaz, opal
- **Lucky Day:** Sunday, Monday, Tuesday, Thursday
- **Power Color:** Black, red, scarlet
- **Lucky Number:** 8, 11, 18, 22

Scorpio is another well-known constellation that has had its place in all major traditions since antiquity. For example, the Babylonians observed the same constellation and referred to it as a scorpion-type creature because of its shape, which resembles a scorpion with a sting, hence the symbolism. The Scorpion's constellation also contains the Antares, a red star referred to in some traditions as "the heart" of the Scorpion and Mars' rival.

Scorpio's quality is fixed, making it the third sign in the zodiac. As usual, this quality provides the sign with stability and endurance. The Scorpion occupies a spot right in the middle of autumn, firmly entrenching it in traits such as reflectiveness, deep thinking, tenaciousness, and the occasional tendency to obsess. Scorpio's fixed quality is somewhat counterbalanced by the sign's water element, which is responsible for the sign's creativity, intuition, and imagination.

Mars rules Scorpio and finds in this sign a nocturnal home, contributing to Scorpio's reserved and secretive nature. Just like Aries, Mars infuses the sign with its combative, confrontational, and aggressive energies, but because Scorpio is a nocturnal home for Mars, these qualities manifest more covertly. In essence, Scorpio can be seen as a quieter, more covert, subtle, and calculated version of the equally aggressive Aries. Detrimental influence can occur when Venus enters the sign due to the planet's peaceful, nurturing energy being at odds with Scorpio's character.

Some of the eclipses will test the intense Scorpio's patience in 2022, but as long as they can harness their calculating, controlled side to weather these storms without getting into too much conflict, the Scorpion will have much to look forward to later in the year.

Sagittarius – The Archer

- **Date Range**: November 22 – December 21
- **Birthstone**: Turquoise
- **Lucky Day**: Wednesday, Thursday, Friday
- **Power Color**: Blue, light blue
- **Lucky Number**: 3, 7, 9, 12, 21

The Archer symbolizes Sagittarius in the form of the Centaur, which has its roots in Greek mythology. The Greek story is that of Chiron, the legendary teacher and hunter who was also the mentor of the illustrious, legendary hero Achilles. According to the myth, Chiron was the one who taught Achilles arts and archery, setting him on a journey toward his eventual glory in the Trojan War. As a race of mythical creatures, the Centaurs were believed to have many of the Sagittarian traits. Like Centaurs, the Archers focus on looking for the truth, traveling, and learning. Chiron himself was the friendliest and most famous of these half-man, half-horse creatures.

The Archer's mutable quality is one of the things that fuel his highly dynamic, adventurous, restless, and sometimes even reckless nature. Occupying the period just before the start of winter, it's in Sagittarius' nature to know a thing or two about transition and transformation. The sign's fire element is just as important for their bold, adventure-seeking ways, and it's also what makes Archers so direct and at times brutally honest.

Sagittarius is the daytime home of Jupiter, its ruling planet. The Archer's fiery and adaptive qualities are a natural playground for Jupiter's influence, which is allowed to reign free and influence the sign in many beneficial ways. Jupiter is where Archers draw much of their strength, especially their affinity for optimism, enthusiasm, and openness. Some issues might arise when Mercury enters the sign and comes into a detriment.

The ever-lucky influence of Jupiter's domicile will continue to follow Sagittarius in 2022 until the second half when the planet becomes retrograde. This doesn't necessarily mean that the Archer will run into bad luck, but with the temporarily weakened influence of Jupiter, they might have to take on the normal odds with the rest of us.

Capricorn – The Sea-Goat

- **Date Range:** December 22 – January 19

- **Birthstone:** Ruby

- **Lucky Day:** Friday, Tuesday, Saturday

- **Power Color:** Dark blue, brown, black

- **Lucky Number:** 4, 8, 13, 22

The Sea-Goat, the symbol of Capricorn and its constellation, goes back to the mythology of numerous civilizations. For the Babylonians, Capricorn was embodied in a Sea-Goat called Ea, who was believed to be the protector of water, creation, and knowledge. Capricorn was also very important in Greek mythology, where it was associated with Amalthea, the legendary goat that nursed Zeus while he was still small and weak after escaping his cannibalistic, murderous father, Cronos.

The Sea-Goat is the final cardinal sign, which heralds the beginning of winter and draws the usual influences of initiative, leadership, and assertiveness from this position. Capricorns can be highly authoritative and respected. These traits are further deepened by the sign's earth element, making the Sea-Goat no stranger to power and control over situations and people.

Capricorn is ruled by Saturn, to which it provides a nocturnal home in exchange for influences of discipline and authority. Saturn in Capricorn also infuses the individual with a strong sense of responsibility and duty. Capricorns have no problem exerting influence on their environment and making things flow in the direction they feel is right. A potentially detrimental influence occurs if the moon enters the sign at birth. Traits such as sensitivity, protectiveness, and a willingness to allow the vulnerability of oneself, which the moon bestows upon Cancers, are mostly lost on Capricorns.

As a Capricorn, you might want to enter 2022 with the awareness that your ruling planet, Saturn, will enter another sign, Aquarius. This means that Capricorns should try not to get too caught up in their leadership role and obsess over the image they project to other people. 2022 will bring many opportunities for Capricorns to indulge in a bit of soul-searching and introspection.

Aquarius – The Water Bearer

- **Date Range:** January 20 – February 18
- **Birthstone:** Garnet
- **Lucky Day:** Thursday, Friday, Tuesday, Monday
- **Power Color:** Sky Blue
- **Lucky Number:** 4, 7, 11, 22, 29

Aquarius is a particularly famous constellation and one of the first in the zodiac to be revered in ancient times. The association with the Water Bearer, just like the mythology surrounding it, dates back to the Babylonians and the protector-god Ea, also associated with Capricorns. Ea was often portrayed as carrying a vase full of overflowing water. Aquarius was also very important for the Egyptians, whose civilizational development and success owed much to the Nile. This river, characterized by its life-supporting habit of overflowing and naturally irrigating the surrounding fertile land along its banks, shares much with the mythical Water Bearer.

Aquarius has a fixed quality and is the last of these signs, situated in the middle of winter. Its air element mitigates the sign's deeply entrenched seasonal position and quality. The air element is why Aquarius is still capable of innovative thinking, inventiveness, improvisation, and other ways of staying ahead of the curve and safe from inertia.

This is the sign where ruling Saturn finds a diurnal home, where Saturn's traits of scrutiny, perceptiveness, and discerning nature fit right in with the Water Bearer's wonderful mind. This is why Aquarians, especially born with Saturn in the sign, will almost always do so well in intellectual, academic, and scientific pursuits. In Aquarius, the sun is in detriment when it enters, limited by the discipline, boundaries, and stern judgment of Aquarius.

2022 has the potential to be the year of many monumental pursuits for the justice-loving Aquarius. The kind Aquarians should beware of their commitment to such pursuits and make sure they don't become obsessed. 2022 promises much to Aquarians regarding finances and romance, which is all the more reason for the Water Bearers out there to pay attention to their personal lives, lest they miss out on important opportunities.

Pisces – The Fish

- **Date Range:** February 19 – March 20
- **Birthstone:** Amethyst
- **Lucky Day:** Thursday, Tuesday, Sunday
- **Power Color:** Sea green, purple, violet
- **Lucky Number:** 3, 9, 12, 15, 18, 24

Symbolized by the Fish, Pisces has been an important constellation for civilizations across the world and throughout the millennia. Poseidon and Neptune, respectively the Greek and Roman gods of the sea, were associated with Pisces. Associations also exist with the Hindu deity Vishnu, with Jesus Christ, and the old Sumerian goddess Inanna. The symbol of the Fish comes from the Latin translation of the word "Pisces" and another mythological association from ancient Greece. In some myths, the Pisces constellation represents the legendary koi fish that saved the lives of Aphrodite and Eros from Typhon, the mythological sea monster. This great service to the gods resulted in the two fishes being given an eternal place among the stars.

Pisces is the last of the zodiac signs and the final mutable sign, to which it owes its adaptability and comfort in change. At the end of winter, the sign's position works in unison with elemental water to further strengthen the Fish's dynamic, adaptable nature. Pisces is also the nocturnal home of Jupiter, its ruling planet, which gets along well with the Fish's intuitive, thoughtful, and introspective personality. However, Mercury tends to be in detriment when it enters the sign of Pisces. This is because of the Fish's willingness to break down barriers and expand, unlike Virgo, the preferred home of Mercury.

If you are a Pisces, you'll find 2022 to be refreshing in many ways, especially after you alleviate the stresses of some of the duties and burdens you've been carrying for a while. Just like Aquarius has an alternative, the modern ruler is Uranus, Pisces has the same in Neptune. This is why Neptune's retrograde that's set to occur in 2022 might cause some turbulence, but certainly, nothing that the intuitive and reflective Pisces can't handle.

Chapter 3: A Clearer Picture of Your Birth Chart

One of the most important aspects of thorough astrological readings is your birth chart. Essentially, this serves to create an outline of all the astrological influences affecting you and your life. In the previous chapter, you learned about some of the pieces that make up the birth chart puzzle, but this chapter will go into more detail on what birth charts are, why they're important, and what they're made of. Your birth chart is a highly personalized overview of astrological influences, which is very specific to your life and the circumstances of your birth. Before we get on with the 2022 forecasts, this chapter will give you an understanding of the fundamentals of birth charts.

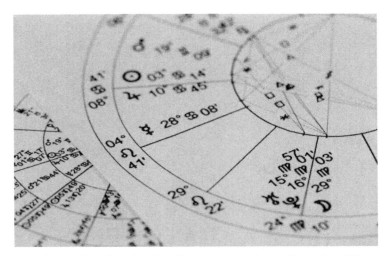

It's worth noting that birth charts are quite a broad subject, given the amount of information they can show about your astrological influences, life, mentality, strengths, weaknesses, and much more. This is why birth charts warrant further study, and the topic is worthy of multiple books. While this chapter will help you grasp the basics, this information will best serve you as a basis for further research.

A birth chart (also referred to as a natal chart) is essentially an astrological map showing where the planets were positioned at the moment of your birth. In the simplest terms, you can consider your birth chart an astrological photograph of the sky above at the moment of your birth. Various events can have their natal charts, such as the beginning of a business venture, relationship, or anything else you can think of, but for our purposes, the focus will be on your birth. The planets of the solar system and the luminaries (the sun and the moon) all play key roles in putting together your birth chart, providing a detailed and unique chart that can tell you much about how you are and why. Apart from providing valuable analysis of one's personality, a birth chart also tells plenty about a person's life and what the future might have in store.

Your birth chart is determined based on three crucial bits of information, the date, exact time, and place of your birth. Based on this information, you can have a personal birth chart created by a professional astrologer or make one yourself with many tools that are available online for free. Creating the chart is one piece of the puzzle while the other is interpretation, which also tends to produce very personal and specific conclusions for individual charts and the individuals they belong to. With the tools mentioned earlier, which often rely on powerful software, you can often get your chart interpreted. Keep in mind that birth charts can also be created based on just two or even one of the three crucial bits of birth information, but these charts will always be less detailed and accurate.

Houses

The most common house system used in contemporary Western astrology is the Placidus system. Houses are a system that divides the horoscope into twelve "houses" determined by the exact time and location of a certain event, in this case, birth. This is because houses are determined based on Earth's rotation and a division of the ecliptic plane of the sun's orbit into twelve parts. These are the twelve equal parts or zones that you usually see dividing up the zodiac, and each of them influences a certain aspect of your life. The twelve houses are numbered counterclockwise, starting with the cusp of the first house, which is also the ascendant sign.

- The First House, also referred to as the House of Self, can be seen as the house of "firsts." The origin of the self makes up who you are, and it governs the way you present yourself to the world and interact with it. The First House is where your identity comes from while also influencing the fate of various endeavors you might undertake. Aries rules this house.

- The Second House is known as the House of Possessions, which indicates the area of life that this house governs. The Second House governs overall stability in your life, income, and immediate surroundings. Beyond the material side of things, this house affects your self-esteem and value system. The Second House is associated with Taurus.

• The Third House is called the House of Communication, and it affects the way you communicate with others and how you relate to yourself, particularly the way you think. This house can influence how you operate in communities, teams, and, of course, your family. This house is the home of Gemini.

• The Fourth House, also known as the House of Family and Home, is ruled by Cancer. Apart from its self-explanatory role, the Fourth House also gives us roots and a sense of belonging, security, trans-generational continuity, and care. This house and its influence determine how nurturing you are as well.

• The Fifth House, ruled by Leo, is the House of Pleasure. This house affects creation in all its forms, from procreation to art and all manner of creativity and expression. As its name suggests, the Fifth House also includes leisure, pleasure, entertainment, and anything else you enrich your life with.

• The Sixth House is the House of Health, and Virgo occupies it. Of course, this house is the one that energizes our strength, vitality, and good health. It's also considered the source of courage, a sense of duty, and self-improvement. This means self-care in all forms and the development of new skills.

• The Seventh House, known as the House of Balance, is home to Libra. In a broader sense, this house governs partnerships and the ability to cooperate with others. This relates to business, family, and any other area of life where it might be important to be diplomatic and agreeable. This is the house of equilibrium.

• The Eighth House is the House of Transformation, ruled by Scorpio. Just like its affiliated sign, the house has an aura of mystery and darkness, as it primarily deals with the cycle of death and rebirth. Other areas of life affected by this house include sexual relationships, commitments, and finances, especially when other people are involved. The house is also associated with regeneration and personal transformation or change.

- The Ninth House is the home of Sagittarius and is otherwise known as the House of Purpose. As can be gathered from its name, this house has implications for a very wide range of things in life. Wisdom, intuition, a sense of the big picture, higher learning, philosophy, and personal growth are only some of the things associated with this house.

- The Tenth House often propels the individual forward, as it is the House of Enterprise. Occupying the very top of the chart, this house governs the authority of all sorts, ambition, motivation, and various human endeavors that have to do with governance and structure. Capricorn rules the house.

- The Eleventh House is associated with Aquarius and is also called the House of Blessings. Among other things, this house pertains to groups that people form, in the broadest sense. The house is also related to an ability to fit in, love, and have one's wishes come true. The house is also often associated with wealth.

- The Twelfth House is the last part of the zodiac and is known as the House of Sacrifice, fitting for its associated sign of Pisces. Just like Pisces, the Twelfth House is associated with intuition, but it's also strongly associated with endings and conclusions in the broadest sense. The finality of all things is what this house helps us deal with.

Planets

All of the planets and the two luminaries each have specific qualities that they bring to the table, and these influences play another crucial part in your birth chart. We've briefly touched upon some of those influences in the previous chapter, but we'll now take a closer look at the energies of these celestial bodies. The way these planets are lined up and positioned when you are born makes all the difference, and it's important to analyze how they relate to each other at that moment. Sometimes, the planets can appear close together, even stuffed into a single constellation. In other cases, they can be spread out very far apart, and that distance is an important astrological factor. All planets and luminaries have five essential dignities: domicile/detriment, exaltation/fall, triplicity, terms (bounds), and face (decan).

- The sun determines the zodiac sign that most people know you by or ask for when they inquire. When you're born, the sun will occupy a particular place in the sky, and the constellation it's the closest to will be your sun sign. The sun and its energy symbolize the very core of our beings, including our ego, self, personality, and everything else that makes us who we are. Like other planets and the moon, the sun has a sign that it rules, which is Leo. The sun is exalted, or at its strongest, in the sign of Aries.

• The moon has plenty of its important physical influences on our planet, such as tides and giving off sunlight. In astrology, it's mostly associated with our feelings and all the things that make up our inner world. In that regard, the moon's symbolism is the opposite of the sun, which represents everything we show and radiate toward the outside world. The moon is the ruler of Cancer, and much of its symbolism reflects in Cancer's sensitive, protective, and nurturing nature. The moon is exalted in Taurus.

• As the smallest planet and the one closest to the sun, Mercury rules Gemini and Virgo while also being exalted in Virgo. In Roman mythology, Mercury was seen as a messenger of the gods. Therefore, it's no accident that Mercury is the planetary symbol of communication in astrology. Mercury's energy is one of intellect, reason, logic, and curiosity that fuels analytical minds.

• Venus is one of the most beloved influences in astrology, being a planet of beauty, love, harmony, affection, and abundance. Ancient Romans saw this planet as the celestial symbol of the goddess of love and beauty. Venus is exalted in Pisces, and it also governs romantic relationships and attraction while affecting several other relationships. This planet rules Libra and Taurus, which perfectly represent the cerebral and physical sides of Venus' sensibility, respectively.

• Mars is another renowned astrological influence, known far and wide as the warrior among the planets, in line with its mythological significance in ancient Rome. Action, aggression, confidence, determination, and other qualities that fuel our fire are all Mars' domain, which shows in the planet's rulership of Aries and Scorpio. Mars is exalted in Capricorn.

• Jupiter is the giant of our solar system and an important astrological influence in our lives. The ancient Greeks considered Jupiter to be Zeus because of its imposing size. This planet rules Sagittarius and Pisces and is exalted in Cancer, governing things like luck, philosophy, abundance, and all things spiritual. Jupiter's energy is an expansive one, always driving us to broaden our horizons and grow, which is an energy that serves the adventurous Sagittarius well.

• Saturn is another gas giant, although not quite as imposing as Jupiter. Apart from the signs of Capricorn and Aquarius, Saturn governs things like limits, time, and rules. Saturn's energy fuels human virtues such as hard work, resilience, and dedication, but it can sometimes be a cold and distant influence. However, this is simply a manifestation of Saturn's emphasis on rules and regulations. Ancient Romans considered Saturn to be the father of civilization, order, and conformity. This planet is exalted in Libra.

• Uranus is one of the planets discovered in the modern era, just like Neptune and Pluto. This makes these planets a bit different than the rest in the astrological sense. Uranus represents rebellion, innovation, and progress, which fits with the fact that it was the first planet discovered with a telescope. In modern Astrology, Uranus rules Aquarius and is exalted in Scorpio. Unlike Saturn, the energy of Uranus is all about rule-breaking and pushing boundaries.

• Neptune was named after the Roman god of the sea, and its energy is shrouded in an aura of mystery, unfathomable vastness, magic, and peculiar spirituality. Neptune rules Pisces in modern astrology and is exalted in Leo. This planet bolsters our imagination, and its energy is a particularly creative one.

• Pluto, often stripped of its planetary title these days, plays an important role in astrology. In the modern sense, the planet rules Scorpio and is exalted in Virgo. Pluto represents transformation, power, regeneration, as well as destruction, and is associated with the underworld. It was named after the Roman god of the underworld, the equivalent of the Greek god Hades. Just like the sign it rules, Pluto is a mysterious, dark influence that has a way of infiltrating itself and affecting important changes in subtle ways.

Planetary Aspects and Nodes

When looking at your birth chart, you'll notice a set of lines that connect the planets in the wheel at different angles. These lines are known as planetary or astrological aspects, and the five most important ones include conjunction, sextile, square, trine, and opposition. The aspect depends on the angle at which the two planets are linked, such as 180 degrees when they are in opposition or zero degrees in conjunction.

The importance of a planetary aspect is in the fact that it represents a sort of partnership or link between two planets. This means that these two planets will be working together, combining their influences for even more powerful effects in your life. When two planets are connected in this way, the reading of the planetary aspect will depend on the sign that the planets occupy and the qualities, energies, and traits of these planets and signs. Of course, this is where birth chart reading gets a bit complicated and can overwhelm a beginner, but that's completely natural. Astrology is a field of study that people can dedicate their entire lives to mastering.

These readings tend to be highly personal and specific to the exact astrological conditions accompanying your birth. The only way to learn what the planets have to say about your life is to take a thorough look at your own birth chart and interpret it on your own or with someone's help. The first step toward reading a birth chart on your own is to learn about the individual characteristics of the zodiac signs, planets, and luminaries, which you have now covered.

Another important detail that plays a part in your birth chart consists of lunar nodes, including the north and south nodes. In the simplest terms, the nodes determine things like purpose and goals in one's life. The nodes tell the birth chart reader these things based on how the ecliptic was moving when you were born and where its axis was.

The North Node is all about what you're learning in this life, be it a skill, a new language, or anything else you're trying to master. This knowledge that you gather also consists of life lessons and morals that you pick up along the way. The North Node is associated with your main purpose in life. Directly opposite of this node is your South Node, which relates to past lives in the cycle of rebirth. It's associated with concepts similar to karma and the lessons and knowledge of past lives. In a way, the South Node determines which parts of this elusive legacy we bring into our current life.

Chapter 4: Important Astrological Events

As you can see, the movements, positions, and other qualities of the planets and luminaries in the sky are the very core of astrological reading. Various movements, positions, and other things happening with these celestial bodies are considered astrological events to be interpreted. These events can be broken down into a few categories, including retrogrades, alignments, eclipses, and various shifts. While we've already mentioned numerous events in our previous discussions, this chapter will take a closer look at our new year and specifically go over the most important astrological events that can be expected each month. These will be the events directly affecting our lives and determining so much when it comes to each individual's astrological fate in 2022.

January

January brings two astrologically important dates and a couple of smaller events that will play a role in everyone's astrological outlook. On January 1, Jupiter will enter the sign of Pisces, where it will remain until May 9. Jupiter's expansive energy's entrance into the magnanimous and compassionate Pisces will spell a mood of giving and compassion at the start of the year.

On the next day, January 2, a new moon will commence in Capricorn, marking a good time to develop new plans and goals. This is because this particular new moon will harness Capricorn's virtues of ambition and common sense. January 2 will be a good day to make long-term plans.

The next important date comes on January 14, beginning the first of Mercury's four retrogrades this year, lasting until February 3. This means that Mercury will be moving backward, at least from our earthly perspective, affecting things like travel, communication, and economic cooperation. This season necessitates caution in all endeavors, especially if you are forced to make big, decisive steps. A patch of good news came on January 29, with Venus exiting its ongoing retrograde, which it had started in December of 2021. This means that the planet of love will be ending its retrograde just ahead of Valentine's Day, which is a very favorable turn of events for all things romance-related.

February

Mercury's first retrograde will end on February 3, bringing some respite to those affected. Beyond this point, you can breathe a sigh of some relief as communication returns to normal.

Another big date is February 20 due to the return of Pluto. This rare astrological event happens only once in 248 years, which will make this return the first one in the history of the United States. Being the most distant planet or planetoid orbiting the sun, Pluto takes a long time to finish its revolution, but when it does, the astrological implications of the event are substantial. The ramifications of this influence might be felt in various parts of the world, manifesting as unrest, major reassessment, and dramatic change. These changes can signify an end for entire systems and the emergence and creation of new ones. Some countries might simply go through deep reforms in the absence of outright revolutions.

All of this might also manifest on the personal level in the lives of individuals. The return of Pluto might be a good opportunity for starting on a great new endeavor or making important, long-term decisions. Starting a new business, taking a step toward self-improvement, or letting go of weight in your life can all be good decisions to make on this day.

March

March first brings the entrance of both Mars and Venus into Aquarius on March 6, bringing up the themes of love, independence, and all the compromises we make in between. The energy of Mars will be that of individualism and forcefulness, clashing with the loving and affectionate energy of Venus, and this struggle will occur right in Aquarius. This can lead to moments of improvisation or a readjustment of expectations and boundaries in a relationship, especially for Aquarius.

March 20 will bring the spring equinox, meaning that day and night in the Northern Hemisphere will be of equal length. This decisive date heralds the tipping of scales in daylight's favor, with days outshining the ever-shortening nights that from this point on. With the growing domination of the sun over the moon, this date marks the beginning of a period for blossoming and becoming active. It's a time of renewal and hope, energizing us all for new victories. Jupiter and Mercury will form conjunction the following day, combining these two energies to make very favorable conditions for travel, openness, and novelty. It's a time for new opportunities and fresh beginnings that come just in time for spring in the Northern Hemisphere.

April

Apart from April Fools' Day, the first of April will bring a new moon in Aries, making this a great time for new beginnings. If you've been mulling over a new business venture or a change of some sort, early April will certainly be a good time to get started with these plans. This translates to relationships, which can benefit from the ambition this new moon brings, just as much as career and business can.

April 12 will be another important date because of the conjunction between Jupiter and Neptune, which will occur in Pisces. This happens only once every 13 years, and the ramifications can be substantial, so it's an opportunity you don't want to miss. This conjunction represents a transit of optimism and idealism with strong themes of beliefs and values. It's a time to grow as a person and make valuable adjustments to your belief system.

On April 26, something called a stellium will occur when three or more planets enter the same sign or house. Stelliums are powerful events that create potent energy clusters that can be very influential. This particular stellium will occur in Pisces and involve Jupiter, Neptune, Venus, the Moon, Mars, and even Juno, which is an asteroid. Astrologists interpret this stellium as highly favorable for all things love-related.

Rounding off this highly eventful month, Pluto will begin its retrograde on April 29, and there will be a partial solar eclipse on April 30, which will coincide with a new moon and occur in Taurus. Pluto's retrograde will last until October 8 and will have associations with death and rebirth. It's an energy that facilitates letting go and moving on. The partial eclipse on April 30 will be another opportunity for fresh, optimistic beginnings.

May

May's first important astrological event comes on May 3 with a sextile aspect between Jupiter and Pluto. The energies produced by this event will bolster our sense of abstraction and abstract thinking ability. It will be a time to visualize, come up with ideas, and dream big, as this sextile brings an increased chance that your dreams and ideas can come to fruition.

Just a day before Jupiter leaves Pisces on May 9, May 10 will mark the beginning of Mercury's second retrograde for the year. This retrograde will pass through Gemini and Taurus, affecting the social and family lives of folks under these signs. If that's you, you would be well advised to exercise more caution in communicating and expressing yourself. This retrograde will end on June 2.

May 16 is another important date because of the full lunar eclipse that's scheduled to occur in Scorpio. The nature of the moon's eclipse, in combination with the nature of Scorpio, has the potential to make folks emotional. This energy might also have a way of bringing repressed, deep-seated feelings to the surface. Scorpios will do well to maintain control and ensure that they don't lash out, and the same applies to some extent to everyone else.

June

A couple of days after Mercury's second retrograde ends, Saturn will begin its own on June 4. As you might recall, Saturn is all about structures, systems, rules, and time, so these aspects of our lives will be affected in some way during this retrograde, which will last until October 23. At this time, it might be a good season to reexamine some of our rules and routines. These considerations apply on the individual level and society as a whole.

Of course, June 21 also has some weight, owing to the summer solstice. As nature blossoms in its fullest abundance, this energy will transfer to our lives as well, marking a good moment for celebration, gratitude, and reflection on the good things in life.

Toward the end of the month, Neptune will begin its retrograde on June 28, which will last until December 3. This retrograde will have implications in our spiritual lives and the potential to reveal secrets, hidden truths, and suppressed feelings. However, it might also be a good season for creative expression, as art can be an excellent way to reveal some hidden truths from within you.

July

The middle of July brings us conjunction between the North Node and Uranus, which will last until the end of the year. Because of the North Node's profound implications for human destiny, the conjunction with the energy of Uranus, which governs change, progress, and liberty, will have far-reaching ramifications. This astrological event is likely to affect the world as a whole, elevating the possibility of dramatic changes. How we deal with these changes and whether we make the best of them will be one of the most important things this year, as it will also set the stage for 2023.

Another conjunction, scheduled for July 16, will be between Mercury and the sun in the sign of Cancer. This event will be a trip down memory lane, toying with your sense of nostalgia and bringing back distant memories of things that had once made you very happy. This might be a good opportunity to rejuvenate old relationships, especially with friends who have grown distant.

The end of the month heralds the entrance of Jupiter into a retrograde on July 28, lasting until November 23. This retrograde might inspire some doubts and a slight loss of confidence in your plans and overall course, so it's going to be important to persevere through these second thoughts.

August

In late August, Uranus is scheduled to go into a retrograde on the 25th, bringing its rebellious energy into a new mode, inspiring innovation, and leading to turbulences that might turn out to be more productive than detrimental. New, unconventional paths might present themselves, and the only question will be whether you are prepared to take risks and gamble on such experiments. This retrograde will carry on into 2023, ending on January 23.

A new moon will begin in Virgo on August 27, which will benefit this sign's sense of duty and organization while providing much of the same for the rest of us. It'll be a good time to focus on work and make improvements where the need is, as well as start on a new project. If you're having problems managing your time, this new moon is a good opportunity to optimize your schedule, rearrange priorities, send out applications for a job, volunteering, or anything else you might find worthwhile or fulfilling.

September

Mercury's third retrograde for the year will begin on September 9 and last until October 2. This retrograde will occur in the signs of Virgo and Libra, which can result in a diminished ability to work efficiently, make decisions, communicate, and stay focused on your work. Simply put, your productivity is likely to be impacted, especially if you're a Virgo or Libra, but don't be too hard on yourself because the retrograde will pass soon enough. However, it's a good idea to adapt to the new reality, so if you notice things aren't going your way when it comes to organization and work, it might be a good idea to get some help or simply postpone some of your workloads if possible. Patience will be a great virtue and friend to you during this time.

Another important event this month will be the autumn equinox, which comes on September 23. Night and day will become equal at this point, bringing a degree of stability and calm. This isn't just because of the equinox, but also due to the onset of autumn and colder weather in the northern hemisphere. There might be a sense of serenity at this point in the year, allowing you to slow down a bit, catch your breath, reflect on learned lessons, and enjoy some of the fruits of your labor.

October

After Mercury's third retrograde ends on October 2, there won't be many important astrological events until later in the month. On October 25, for instance, we're looking at a partial solar eclipse coinciding with a new moon in Scorpio. Scorpio's energy will be strong during this time, and it will be a particularly favorable period for articulating your emotions and getting some relief if you find yourself struggling with emotional turmoil before that time. Hopefully, these changes should make for a more relaxed, comfortable Halloween this year.

As the Halloween season is underway, Mars will enter its retrograde on October 30. Excitements will die down as Mars' energy diminishes for a while, but this might be just the thing we all need to take a step back, sit down, and relax for a bit while contemplating matters relating to our careers. As Mars reduces the energy it injects into our ambition, we might find this a good time to reconsider some of our goals and desires. During this time, some you might even realize that your career isn't the most important thing in the universe, allowing you to focus on other aspects of your life for a while. The retrograde of Mars will go on until January 12.

November

November 8 marks the final, full lunar eclipse of 2022, happening in Taurus. This will be a time for closure as well as rebuilding. As is often the case with eclipses, they provide an opportunity to let go and close certain chapters of our lives that have become burdensome. Whether it's a relationship or some other stressful undertaking, perhaps November 8 will be the time to consider pulling the plug. However, you must be careful not to act too soon in that regard because this eclipse will also make it easier to rebuild bridges and mend long-standing issues in relationships. Based on the particularities of your relationship, you'll have to decide which course to take.

A couple of days before Jupiter's retrograde ends on November 23, November 21 brings important conjunction between Mercury and Venus in the sign of Sagittarius. This turn of events will be favorable for romantic endeavors and strengthen existing relationships for Sagittarians and others alike.

December

The last month of 2022 starts with the end of Neptune's retrograde on December 3. Another important event will follow on December 9 when Venus and Jupiter will form a square aspect while occupying Sagittarius and Pisces, respectively. This day would be well used to reflect on past experiences and lessons regarding love and relationships, particularly if such lessons can benefit an ongoing relationship. It's a good idea to take some time to relax, reminisce, and consider your next steps on this front.

The year will end with the beginning of Mercury's fourth and final retrograde on December 29, which will last until January 18. This might provide for a confusing end to a year, but it won't be something that can throw you too far off the balance if you stay the course and brace yourself. Just remember not to make any rash decisions and instead try to enjoy the New Year's celebrations as laid back as you can be.

Chapter 5: Love and Relationships

Considering the planets' positions and the astrological events through the months of 2022 that we've just covered, we'll now take a closer look at what each of the zodiac signs can expect. This chapter will focus on relationships and how the planets might influence how you relate to and interact with people in your life, including new and already established contacts.

The aforementioned Venus retrograde early in the year warrants some caution in romantic endeavors. This will change by January 29, when Venus positions itself firmly in Capricorn and opens us up for romance. This can mean starting a new relationship or spicing up an existing one. Jupiter and Uranus will form a sextile on February 17 before Jupiter forms a conjunction with Neptune on April 12, all of which will provide good conditions for romance and friendship. The solar eclipses in late April and October, respectively in Taurus and Scorpio, will also provide opportunities for connection. Another important moment for relationships will be on May 3 due to the sextile relationship that will form between Jupiter and Pluto.

Aries

If you're an Aries who already has important relationships to cherish, then maintaining and strengthening those relationships will be the name of the game for you in 2022. An opportunity for a new special someone might appear, but 2022 will best be used to renew and improve other important relationships in your life. This applies to friends and family alike. It can also be a good year to adopt a pet, which will provide you with companionship and potential opportunities for new human contacts.

If you've noticed yourself going through profound changes in the past year, then you might be ripe for novelties in your love life. It's likely that these changes have opened you up more than before and have stoked an appetite for stability, which a serious relationship might provide. Indeed, if your existing relationships are squared away and fully blossoming, then 2022 will undoubtedly be as good of a year as any to strike up something new. However, it's important to maintain your standards and boundaries to ensure that any new relationship will stand up to scrutiny. The final months of 2022 might bring additional changes in your love life and provide fertile ground for serious commitments. Big things might happen in October and November, so be ready to make the best of them.

Taurus

2022 will be all about reevaluation, adjustment, and compromise for the Taureans and their relationships. This also means a reexamination of priorities and expectations so you can better understand what it is that matters the most to you. These questions will be important precisely because of the high likelihood that you'll have to make compromises. As early in the year as possible, a Taurean should know exactly what they are willing to compromise and what's off the table. While analyzing your relationships, another important question to ask this year is how much you're giving and what you're taking. Strong relationships tend to be built on a foundation of give-and-take, and when this balance is lacking, it might be time for adjustments.

Big questions aside, 2022 should be a very good year for new romances in the world of Taurus. You might find the stars especially inclined toward your romantic endeavors in January, June, and July. Despite the tough decisions some of you might have to make, you'll find that 2022 will provide ample opportunity for passion, particularly thanks to the influence of Uranus. If you were born in early May, you might be especially lucky in this regard. You'll likely run into Scorpio, Pisces, or Leo in unexpected, new romantic chapters. Beyond the romance, Taureans can expect Mars to lead them into valuable family reunions in July and August.

Gemini

Geminis might run into a bit of occasional turbulence when it comes to relationships in 2022. Romance has all the potential to blossom in the new year. Still, you would be well advised to exercise more caution and care in how you treat your loved ones, as existing relationships might require some maintenance. Geminis might be prone to set their expectations too high this year, so you should be careful not to exhaust the people you care about.

Concerning social life in the broadest sense, Geminis have a lot to look forward to, thanks to numerous social events that are likely to happen. Autumn will be a time for romance, with a tiny bit of turbulence having to do with feelings of jealousy. In the worst-case scenario, you'll encounter opportunities to learn valuable lessons that can help you search for a meaningful relationship if such is lacking in your life. April 30 will be a good day for making long-term relationships official if you plan to get married. In general, April, May, and October will be the months with favorable romantic conditions for Gemini, especially when starting new relationships.

Cancer

On the romantic side of things, Cancers, too, should have a very good year in 2022. Many positive, refreshing changes can be expected this year, whether you are single or already in a relationship. The new moon starting on January 17 will be particularly influential in this regard. Still, because it heralds a major change and something new, it might also spell the end of some relationships. In some situations, this might not even be a bad thing, especially because June 29 will bring a new cycle in which love should blossom for you.

Single Cancers can look forward to great opportunities for love between January and March and then again from July to September. Cancers being Cancers. However, it will be very important to stay communicative and open to these opportunities, assuming that a relationship is something you long for. Old flames might rekindle loves that were thought to be forgotten, with an old partner showing up unexpectedly in your life at some point in 2022. Should such an opportunity arise, Cancers will have important decisions to make. The entrance of Venus into Cancer in July will elevate the odds of a passionate romantic encounter, especially if you find yourself on vacation. Should such a new opportunity coincide with the reemergence of a past partner, Cancers will have to see which direction they want to go.

Leo

2022 has the potential to be a year of fresh beginnings and important changes for Leos when it comes to relationships, romance included. As long as Leos are prepared to embrace changes, love could blossom to a great extent in 2022. This year will also be a time to let go, to release the baggage some Leos have been struggling with for a while. Whether it's a toxic relationship, past trauma, or an unhealthy obsession, 2022 will be a great year for you to let go and enjoy a fresh new start. Wiping the slate clean is hardly ever easy, but the planets in 2022 will give Leos enough strength to do so if they make up their minds.

Outgoing Leos who find themselves single will have many opportunities to look forward to. January, March, July, and November should be particularly fruitful in regard to romance. On the other hand, if you are already in a relationship, it will be good to try your best to be more honest as it could greatly benefit and strengthen your relationship. This holds true for romance and friendship alike. The moon will play an important role in Leo's love life on February 16 and August 12, the perfect opportunity to embrace new contacts and let go of toxic ones.

Virgo

2022 might prove to be a crucial year on the path toward marriage for many Virgos. This can mean getting married, of course. Still, it might also entail a new acquaintance that will lead to a long-term relationship and eventually marriage. Nonetheless, Virgos meeting a new love interest should exercise caution in 2022, as they might be prone to misjudging people and eventually running into some unpleasant surprises. As long as you make double sure that you haven't gotten the wrong idea about someone, you'll have great opportunities to look forward to, especially in April and September.

Virgos will find themselves becoming more affectionate and open-hearted on all fronts in the new year. This can translate to great experiences in love, friendship, family, and all sorts of partnerships. In fact, 2022 might be the year when a Virgo could meet their soul mate, romantically or otherwise. Virgos who have children or grandchildren will get more joy out of them in 2022 than ever before, especially during the summer. Your familiar relationships might require more attention and time in 2022, but this commitment will produce great results, bring you many reasons to rejoice, and set you up for long-term stability on this front.

Libra

For Libras, 2022 might be the year when friendships blossom beyond what was expected, eventually turning into a romantic relationship. It seems that the planets have major plans in 2022 for Libras in the realm of love and relationships, in general. July will be particularly intense, with great potential for major changes and numerous opportunities that might land you in a situation where you have to make choices.

Still, it will be important for Libras to focus on their internal struggles and ensure that these issues don't persist and spill over into their love life. If this happens, it might hamper your ability to make the most of the abundant romantic opportunities that 2022 will bring. Before you build a relationship, make sure that you have sorted out any potential issues with self-respect and feelings of self-worth. Periods between April and June and September to November will be particularly productive for the love lives of Libras. The influence and movement of Jupiter on June 10 will herald the beginning of an especially favorable period for existing relationships that might last up to a year. Romantic transitions can also be a predominant theme for some Libras, meaning marriage, break-ups, and new beginnings.

Scorpio

Scorpios, too, will encounter opportunities on the love front, and 2022 might be a good year to lay back, take it easy, and simply consider some options. On the other hand, many Scorpios will find extended periods of solitude highly beneficial this year, as this time alone will allow them to acclimate themselves to changes. If you've been having trouble in your love life, then you can breathe a sigh of relief as 2022 is very likely to turn the tide in your favor. A new sense of self-appreciation and self-worth will attract new people and improve existing relationships. Still, the important takeaway is that Scorpios must not forget their valuable alone-time in 2022, despite how social the year might turn out. April, May, and November will be great months for a Scorpio's romance.

Interesting revelations might also come in the form of someone close to you confessing their love, which might be exactly how a new relationship starts for you. Come August. However, Scorpios will feel the need to withdraw for a while, which is always a great way to process the opportunities presented to them and make the best decision possible.

Sagittarius

When it comes to relationships, 2022 might turn out to be a mixed bag for Sagittarius. This year will be the year of serious decisions and major commitments for Archers on the romantic front. Existing relationships are likely to take a more serious turn, and Sagittarians will be well advised to prepare themselves for these changes. Simply put, now is the time for you to get serious and prepare for moments of truth. This can have different outcomes, depending on your situation. Some Archers will settle down with a new, serious partner, while others will take their existing relationships to the next level. For others, however, getting serious might entail breaking off a relationship if it proves to be a waste of time and emotions. Such a decisive moment might come around June 14.

Things might be somewhat dodgy with family life, particularly when it comes to your relationship with some older family members. Disagreements might arise, and certain decisions you make might run into disapproval, but you'll do well to persevere and stay the course, as you are likely to be proven right in the end. 2022 will also be a year for letting go and healing residual pains. This might mean fixing a relationship in crisis, letting go of a toxic one, or even reviving a relationship from the past.

Capricorn

2022 will be a very good year for Capricorns in their friendships and familial relationships. These connections will blossom and continue going strong throughout the year. However, in romance, Capricorns might find themselves in long-distance relationships. Such an arrangement might come as a new, distant acquaintance or as a new reality in an ongoing relationship. Depending on your situation and partner, a long-distance relationship might not necessarily be a bad thing, of course.

Capricorns who've been working on self-improvement will begin to pick the fruits of their efforts in 2022. These improvements will positively affect all types of relationships in your life. March, April, and September will bring favorable conditions for romance, in general, and this will be a good time for Capricorns to improve ongoing relationships. You might end up establishing a long-distance relationship with someone on vacation or business trip, even someone from a distant country, resulting in an exotic romance that may or may not last. At any rate, this kind of relationship will bring a degree of affection and joy into your life while not stifling your independence too much. However, if you find yourself wanting to transform such a relationship into a serious, long-term commitment, you'll have to put in the effort.

Aquarius

For Aquarians, 2022 will be a good year for relationships, but you'll be well advised to focus on quality over quantity. This goes double for single Aquarians who long for love and affection and might be too eager to get into a relationship with an unsuitable partner. Make sure that you establish a strong set of boundaries and standards that you'll stick to when choosing who to devote yourself to. It's also possible that an old acquaintance or love might show up out of nowhere and put you on the spot with difficult decisions to make.

Either way, 2022 will be a favorable and productive year for Aquarians searching for love. Luck will be on your side as well, likely putting you in the right place, at the right time, and with the right people. Just remember not to forego your boundaries and rush into a relationship just because you're feeling lonely. Patience is the name of the game, and eventually, it will pay off. Be prepared to make big decisions as well, which can include a whole range of decisive steps concerning your love life.

Pisces

If you're a Pisces, you can expect 2022 to be a year of surprises and unexpected developments, *particularly if you're single and looking to mingle*. The theme will be one of consolidation, improvement, and greater commitment for those already in relationships. Surprises can come from unknown prospects or people from your past, but in either case, it's going to be important for you to follow your renowned intuition and trust your gut while also remaining honest. March, May, and September could be particularly favorable for romance.

Ups and downs might alternate due to misunderstandings in ongoing relationships, so Pisces would be smart to exercise due caution in how they express themselves and what they say. This, however, doesn't necessarily entail compromises, as Pisces should stay true to their principles. May could distinguish itself as a month of intense ups and downs, the result of which will depend on what you make of those situations, for better or worse. December will be the best time to deepen an existing relationship and take your commitments to the next level. Whether you end up taking steps toward marriage or just decide to devote more care to your partner, you'll certainly remain a loyal and most compassionate partner, as is the nature of Pisces.

Chapter 6: Family and Marriage

Married or not, family life is a crucial aspect of most people's lives, so it's only natural that you'll look to the planets for a bit of insight into what you might expect on this front in 2022. The planets have plenty to tell us about these things, with a few important insights for each of the signs during the coming months. We've touched upon marriage a bit in the previous chapter, but this time we'll put a bit more emphasis on this important part of the human experience, whether it's about future prospects or an ongoing marriage.

Much of what we've discussed thus far applies to marriages and familial relationships in general, so make sure to use the previous forecasts where applicable for your particular situation (marriage, family life, or marital prospects in the future). This chapter will look at marriages and all the accompanying relations in more detail. As is the case with other relationships, the planets in 2022 are poised to bring great changes for many while providing an opportunity to consolidate for others.

Aries

2022 can be a year of strengthened bonds and increased closeness for already-married Rams. Communication and understanding on a deeper, more intimate level will improve between you and your partner throughout the year. Even if you run into some turbulence and misunderstandings, these tests will only serve to strengthen your marriage.

In general, 2022 will be a particularly good year for kindness and increased affection on your part. Every extra bit of attention, affection, or any other way of going the extra mile for your spouse or any other family member is likely to leave a strong, lasting impact for the better. Your loved ones will pay attention, and every extra bit of attention you show will not go unappreciated or ignored. Before long, you might find that your goodness is reciprocated. This doesn't necessarily mean saying nice things or buying presents for the important people in your life. In fact, the time you spend with these folks might prove to be a much more valuable commodity. Your important relationships will benefit greatly from any extra time you spend with your loved ones this year.

Taurus

This year will be eventful for Taureans on the family front, just like everywhere else. Some of the improvements and successes you'll see on this front might come as a result of professional successes. Indeed, the connection between these two areas of your life might be quite pronounced at some points in 2022. Overcoming a major professional obstacle, getting that promotion you've wanted, or resolving some situation that might have been a major stressor in your life can lead to less tension on the home front. It can also open up new opportunities for your family, such as travel, moving, or improving your general quality of life.

You might also find that your family is more supportive in 2022, giving you all manner of support that will propel you forward through hardships. For unmarried Taureans who are in committed relationships, 2022 might be the year when you finally tie the knot. This major milestone will fit naturally into the overall theme of self-improvement and accomplishment that will follow you in 2022. Married Taureans will find 2022 very favorable for communication and understanding, which will help you resolve any of the issues your marriage might have been facing. It's going to be all about finding common ground with your partner and your other family members.

Gemini

The blossoming romance that Geminis can expect in 2022 will undoubtedly rub off on any existing marriages. This will be a good year to give your spouse all the special care that enriches life. You can make a special and romantic dinner, take your spouse out for a surprise fancy dinner or event, or book a nice tourist retreat where the two of you can catch up and rejuvenate your relationship. Whatever you do in this regard will have amplified positive effects in 2022, and none of it will be a waste of time. For younger couples, 2022 might also be the year to consider having a child. If you get to work in this department, results should come no later than the year's second half.

Single Geminis must remember the theme of caution and contemplation that will permeate their love lives. By all means, starting a relationship or making an ongoing one more serious is always a welcome change, but if you are considering marriage, you should spend quite a bit of time reflecting and contemplating. You have to consider all the ins and outs of your relationship and ask yourself if your partner is the person you can see yourself spending eternity with.

Cancer

2022 will be a good year for Cancers planning to get married. Existing relationships could blossom to the point where marriage becomes a very real possibility, but even single Cancers might luck out and find a partner who is revealed in short order to be suitable for marriage. This doesn't mean you should get married right away, of course, but this year might indeed mark the beginning of something good and strong, which could get very serious further down the line.

Married Cancers should make an effort to ensure that their communication with the spouse and other family members is on point this year, lest you find yourself in misunderstandings because of your tendency to keep things bottled up. Open up and involve your family in your life. You'll find unending reserves of support in 2022, with your loved ones watching your back and giving you all the help you need in whatever endeavor you embark upon. Communication will trump all other priorities in your family life, and as long as you take care of that front, the year ahead will be very kind to you. This year will also probably bring new opportunities for Cancers who are separated or divorced, giving you a second chance at married life if that's something you've been longing for.

Leo

Married Leos will find 2022 full of love and intimacy with that special someone, with their relationship going strong throughout the year. You can expect to be happy, and a noticeable harmony will permeate your home life and familial relationships. Like Geminis, Leos should have a lot of luck with conceiving a child in 2022, so this might be the year to bring this up with your spouse. Some Leos might run into a couple of issues in their relationships on some occasions in 2022, involving arguments and other minor disagreements. However, with patience and dedication, such challenges will easily be sorted out, bringing you and your partner closer together in the process.

For Leos in relationships, it's worth noting that the second half of the year might not be the best time for proposals. The important thing will be not to rush into marriage. However, recently married Leos will have plenty of stars working for them and their happiness in 2022. In general, Leo's 2022 theme is that love will triumph, making this an overall good year for all things family-related, despite any potential challenges that might come your way. Each challenge will only make your relationships with your loved ones stronger in the end.

Virgo

As briefly mentioned in the previous chapter, 2022 will be a favorable year for Virgos to marry, especially for those already in relationships. All of your relationships will get stronger this year because of your heightened affection and love for those you hold dear. This love will be felt in the air, but you'll also do well to show it through actions, no matter how small or seemingly menial they might be. It's a good year to please the people you care about, so 2022 will bring you plenty of opportunities to take your loved ones out, make them feel special, and just do all those little things that enrich their lives. Your life will only get enriched as a result.

You'll find that your spouse will be very supportive this year, so the more you communicate and talk to them openly, the better. There will be no reason to suppress any grievances this year, as anything that might be bugging you is best brought to the light and sorted out through the joint efforts of you and your loved ones. In general, family life has the potential to bring even more comfort than before and embellish your life this year more than ever before.

Libra

This year holds a lot of potential for Libras who are single and looking for a relationship that they hope might set the foundations for marriage. It will also be a good time if you are already in a relationship and are hoping to take it to the next level. If you find yourself mulling over the idea of proposing to your partner, then it might be time to gather the courage and finally take that step. You'll find that 2022 has good things in store for you.

For married Libras, this is the year when your spouse might require a bit more attention, care, and consideration. Sometimes, it's better to forego certain words and arguments, even if you're convinced that you're right. Think about what you stand to gain by proving yourself to be right – *and consider if it's worth the trouble.* There is no need to raise tensions over petty things, and as long as you keep your cool, the second half of the year should bring far less disagreement and friction. It's also important to remember to include your spouse in the decision-making process around the home as an equal partner instead of just imposing your will.

Scorpio

Unfortunately, married Scorpios will be prone to getting into arguments with their spouse this year, but this is certainly manageable or even fully preventable when you know what to expect. Keep in mind that these influences can manifest as something completely harmless, such as not seeing eye to eye on something related to furniture or similar ordinary aspect of home life. The important thing will be staying patient, controlling yourself, and not blowing things out of proportion, which shouldn't be too difficult for the ever-subtle Scorpio.

Scorpios also can experience some minor judgment and disapproval from their spouses, mostly regarding their lifestyle and minor life choices. Perhaps this will entail some constructive criticism that you should consider objectively. You must remember not to automatically take criticism from your loved ones as a personal attack and leave your ego out of it. If someone who loves you has a few small critiques, they're probably saying that because they have your best interest at heart. Blindly agreeing to everything your family tells you without really considering the substance of what's been said isn't a solution either. Simply put, you should listen wholeheartedly and engage with your loved ones.

Sagittarius

As mentioned earlier, 2022 brings opportunities for Sagittarians to get serious about their relationships and delve deeper into commitment. For many of you in relationships, this can mean marriage. At the very least, it's going to be a good time to subtly bring up the subject and test the waters so that you know where you stand with your partner. Because the planets are inclined toward you, though, the chances are good that ideas of marriage will flow both ways this year. It's best to get on this before September rolls around, but this should by no means suggest that you should be hasty and rush into marriage.

The last few months of 2022 can be a confusing time for Sagittarians, so it's best to avoid getting married at this time – or making any major decisions if you're already married. The most foolproof plan is to take some of that time to relax and spend leisurely time with your loved ones without any heavy emotional lifting.

Capricorn

Single Capricorns who long to get married should put their radars into overdrive in 2022 because there will be quite a few prospects coming your way. As long as you exercise due caution and analysis, you might just meet the perfect match for your long-term commitment. This match might appear where you least expect, and it might even be an unlikely stranger from far away.

Married Capricorns would do well to get involved in some marriage maintenance this year, spend more time with their spouse, and address any open issues. It'll be a great year for traveling, so you might want to plan a little getaway with your spouse or perhaps with the entire family – especially if you're looking to bond with your kids a bit more. This will be a great year to pick the fruits of your emotional investments and enjoy all the finer aspects of family life. It will do you good to take some time to slow down, relax, and take a gander at all you've accomplished. It never hurts to refresh one's perspective and remind yourself of all those things you should be grateful for.

Aquarius

Even though Aquarians might run into quite a few romantic opportunities this year, it might not necessarily be the best year to get married. Communication will be especially important this year if you are to get a solid read on situations having the potential to play a central role in your love life. If you have a problem, you should talk it out, as this alone can save you a whole lot of trouble in 2022.

The same applies to married Aquarians, who would do well to clear the air with their spouses if there are any issues. Your stress might be infringing on your relationship; this is why this will be a good year to pick up some healthy habits and programs like yoga and other types of exercise. Sort out your stressors and get to feeling better. You'll soon find many other things will come easier, including potential misunderstandings in your marriage. Of course, none of the potential turbulence will be insurmountable or devastating, especially if you remember to stay patient and composed. If you navigate these few twists and turns properly, the rest of the year will certainly be as pleasant as ever in regard to your relationships and family life.

Pisces

As we discussed earlier, your love life might be a bit of a bumpy ride this year, with a few unexpected situations, for better or worse. Just like Aquarius, you'll have to be patient and ensure that you communicate and express your needs as effectively and as harmlessly as possible. For married folks, those bumps in the road will provide many opportunities for heart-to-heart conversations that can get to the root of many problems. This is why the potential turbulences of 2022 might be a blessing in disguise, helping you make your relationship stronger than ever.

While this year will likely bring opportunities for new relationships if you are a single Pisces, it's probably not going to be an ideal time for marriage. Instead, you should take your time to really get to know your partner and yourself. If you find someone you think is a suitable lifelong partner, it's perhaps best to give it a trial run by moving in together. That way, it'll be easier to imagine what your life together might look like before you make any official commitments for life.

Chapter 7: Business and Career

Our loved ones come first. Still, many people find that life without intimacy and love can never be fulfilling, even with all the money and professional success in the world. However, careers and professional life are still very important. Work isn't just about money, of course, as it's another area of life where many folks will seek and find fulfillment.

2022 will be the year of many opportunities and options for careers and business, so there is a lot to look forward to. In line with the year's general theme, 2022 will be a year for changes concerning careers and work in general. You'll have motivation, ambition, and opportunities to explore new paths and go off in new directions for your work. Heightened creative energy will also fit very well into this climate.

The year might get off to a somewhat slow start, though, due to that ongoing Venus retrograde, but things will come back to normal starting on January 29. If you've been feeling lethargic and unmotivated in your work, late January is likely to bring a new, positive wind. Beyond that point, it will be a year with ample opportunity for success.

Aries

Aries will be off to a strong start this year with a lot of inspiration, ambition, and drive that's characteristic of this sign. You might find yourself wanting to push all sorts of boundaries and enact changes not just in your life but in your environment as well. The most important thing for Rams in 2022 will be the struggle to retain that initial optimism, drive, and inspiration throughout the year despite any potential adversities. As such, despite some positive forecasts, Rams would be wise to prepare themselves ahead of time for potential turbulence on the professional front.

The overarching problem for Aries in 2022 will be the high potential for disagreements with all sorts of people in your immediate surroundings, especially coworkers and business partners. The important thing, which is the eternal struggle of every Aries, will be to keep your cool, your wits about you, and do your best to communicate even when you and your coworkers are on completely different pages. Patience will pay off in the end as long as you keep your eyes on your main goals that transcend the minor snags of daily life. If you find yourself in unknown territory, pressured by uncertainty, it's a good idea to hold off on major decisions and drastic changes until things clear up.

Taurus

Taureans will quickly recover from any bumps in the road early in the year. The forecasts for this sign are very prosperous and favorable, as 2022 will be the year for the Bulls to get things done, overcome many hurdles, and elevate their careers in the process. On this front, the goal you crave the most might just become a reality in 2022 if you put in the effort, as the planets and stars are undoubtedly in your favor for much of the year.

Even before the ongoing Venus retrograde ends, the connection between the North Node and the Sun that will begin on January 18, for the first time in 18 years, will land Taurus right at the center of business success and good fortune, in general. March 12 will bring even more good fortune thanks to Venus and Mars in Aquarius, which will also be a good time for Taureans to make plans and set new goals. The Jupiter-Neptune conjunction on April 12 will continue this trend, making this the season where the fruits of your labor will be ripe for the picking. In all, 2022 will be the year for you to shine and propel your career to new heights.

Gemini

Gemini is another sign that can expect great things thanks to the conjunction on April 12. Geminis who have been working hard toward a particular goal for a long time can expect those efforts to bear fruit in 2022, and then some. The planets imply a forecast of prosperity and abundance, which is very likely to come as a result of professional growth and advancement.

If your career involves a lot of networking, the contacts you've been making all this time will come into play. They will help you along the way toward your main goals, especially thanks to the influence of Jupiter through Aries in May and December. Similar themes will mark the month of October as Jupiter leaves Aries and enters Pisces. The one thing that Geminis should beware of is stress, especially early in the year. To manage this stress, you might want to adopt new, relaxing activities such as hiking. As long as you manage the stress and persevere through a few potential rough patches, 2022 will be a year with your name on it when it comes to professional life.

Cancer

Those entrances that Jupiter will make into Aries and Pisces will extend a fair share of luck to Cancers. For this reason, Cancers too will have things to look forward to in May, October, and December. You are likely to feel invigorated by these energies at those intervals, giving you the push you need to make your ideas materialize in the real world and get you closer to your goals.

Cancers can benefit a lot in 2022 from creativity, uniqueness, and even edginess in some instances. In essence, you should look into any potential ways of distinguishing yourself from others, especially if they are your competitors. Of course, such efforts should consist of productive and positive actions and remain within the bounds of common sense.

This will be a good year for you to give fresh ideas a try, even if they are a bit radical. The new ideas you might come up with this year might also apply fairly well to your previous endeavors, which can be revisited and made better. All of this can entail some risk, but in the end, it will set you apart from the crowd and earn you respect.

Leo

In 2022, Leos must make sure that they retain the radiating confidence they are so renowned for. There will be moments where that confidence might get shaken and when self-doubt might set in, but Leos will have the strength to surmount such obstacles. Self-perception is just as important for Leos as outside perception is, so if you feel an onset of self-doubt and diminished confidence, it will be best to fix the underlying causes of these issues as soon as possible. As soon as you come back to your confident, fiery self, all else will fall into place soon enough. If such an episode were to arise, it would most likely come in January, after which Leos should be back on track.

Under the influence of the North Node, Leos have a chance of going through some significant changes in their professional lives. You can expect valuable opportunities to come your way, but you'll make the most of them if you spend some time before that in reflection, mulling over the exact direction you want to go in your career. When an opportunity comes, it's going to be important for Lions to know exactly what they want, lest the opportunity slips amid a lack of decisiveness.

Virgo

For Virgos, who have endured struggles in 2021 (going through stress, uncertainties, and instability), 2022 will bring considerable relief. Career progress will feel difficult and somehow hampered in May and June, but these rough patches will be nothing for Virgos to lose sleep over. Doubts will be transient, and soon enough, Virgos will get their slice of the good fortune pie.

Thanks to the influence of Jupiter in early May and late October to December, opportunities will arise for new, more lucrative business relationships. However, it's going to be important for you to maintain relationships with coworkers, as their assistance might prove crucial during the October 30 retrograde of Mars, going into January of 2023. During this time, your progress might be set back somewhat if you cannot get the help you need at the right time. In all, 2022 should be particularly fruitful for Virgos, who are in art, design, and beauty. Make sure that you have someone to lean on, and there will be no amount of turbulence that can kick you off your path toward success.

Libra

Libras can expect a shift in their focus after January, providing the potential for significant changes in their career paths. This can also entail a reshuffling of priorities as you realize that work shouldn't be just about money but also about fulfillment and creativity. Another thing that might affect your career path will be the Venus star point on January 8, which will shower us all with the energy of growth and evolution.

Since the Jupiter-Neptune conjunction on April 12 has the potential to flare up some passions and feelings, beware that you don't become too emotional, as this might cause a rift between you and some coworkers. The entire time leading up to autumn is a good opportunity to continuously hatch your new plans and figure out their lesser details so that you're ready to take action when the time comes. Plans are likely to come to fruition on October 22, thanks to the alignment of the Venus star point and the sun. Throughout 2022, Libras will do well to remember that external approval and validation won't put the food on the table or lead to a more fulfilling professional experience. This year, you'll be better off focusing on your inner struggle than paying attention to naysayers.

Scorpio

In 2022, Scorpios might find that the issues from other areas of their personal lives could spill over into their professional lives and careers. If this should happen, you might find yourself slightly off-balance at times, but any such problems will be easily mended by focusing on your main goals and establishing clear rules and boundaries.

The lunar and solar eclipses on May 16 and October 25, which are happening in Scorpio, will present good opportunities for advancement at your workplace. These are the days when you should consider asking for a raise or bringing up the subject of an expected promotion. This is how Scorpios might start a new chapter in their professional life with more money and added responsibilities that carry weight in a given profession. Late October's retrograde of Mars, however, has the potential to take some steam out of you and slow down your drive and ambition, during which time it'll be a good idea to look for sources of motivation to keep you going. Apart from the main interests of your work, 2022 will also be a good year for personal projects on the side. These might provide you with some fulfillment and enrich your life, but they might also blossom into significant business ventures.

Sagittarius

Like most other signs, Sagittarius, too, will benefit from the energies of Jupiter and Neptune this April. As an Archer, you'll find that the spiritual growth and changes that this year will bring might provide just the right type of fuel to propel your career forward as well. This should come as no surprise since our spirituality always has the potential to affect all the other areas of our life. Your sign's spiritual consolidation in 2022 could also give you the strength to make bold decisions and introduce some drastic changes in your professional life, which could pay off ten-fold in the long term.

Your spiritual maturing and strengthening will reflect in your work, particularly in your creative endeavors, which will emit an aura of inspiration, depth, and sophistication. If you find yourself in a bit of confusion at any point in the first half of the year, with a lack of confidence in the trajectory you've taken, such doubts should dissipate from July 31 onward. You'll have a clearer idea of where you're going and what exactly you should do, allowing you to prepare well for the upcoming Mercury retrograde in September. Beware, as this retrograde can create quite a bit of turbulence in your professional life until October 2 before Venus takes over and begins a season of utmost prosperity and success from October 22 and onward.

Capricorn

Early 2022 will affect Capricorns in much the same way as the rest of the signs. You might start feeling like what you're doing isn't producing results, making you doubt that your efforts have any purpose. However, this will mostly boil down to baseless self-doubt, as it's entirely possible that January might bring some gains in your professional life. The key is not to lose sight of these positive developments, as the ongoing retrograde might make you more inclined toward negative thinking.

Things will start looking up as the year progresses, and in October, Capricorns can expect a rush of confidence as well as new opportunities for promotions and raises. Your renewed confidence will propel you forward and ensure that you are ready to snatch any such opportunities as soon as they crop up, so you should be on the lookout this autumn. In the absence of a promotion, some Capricorns might be presented with a new and better job opportunity around that same time.

Aquarius

Aquarians will be under a particularly strong influence of 2022's eclipses. The eclipses scheduled for this year will invigorate all of your efforts and speed up many aspects of your journey, bringing you ever closer to your most important professional goals. This will be a great year to advance your career or develop and strengthen your business venture. When a lunar eclipse occurs in the professional part of your natal chart on May 16, you'll start having some very good times at work. On top of that, the solar eclipse that's coming on October 25 will mark a great time to start a new business or expand an existing one into new markets.

Simply put, 2022 will be a year of breakthroughs and major achievements for Aquarians, with many crucial milestones passed. The influences of Uranus and the North Node will also be major influences whose energy will be so strong on your professional path that things might even start moving too fast at one point. It's certainly possible to have too many opportunities in life, so you should make sure not to get distracted and lured off course. As long as you know what you want and keep your sights on a particular goal, you'll most certainly make the most of any opportunities you encounter.

Pisces

With many changes and novelties, Pisceans have had an eventful year in 2021 but will find 2022 to be a year of consolidation, prosperity, and fruit picking. Indeed, if you've put in a lot of work during the previous year without seeing much in the way of results, you'll likely have a lot to look forward to in 2022 as those efforts slowly but surely begin producing results.

Unexpected developments might land you in a world of confusion at times, which is why it's going to be important to plan ahead and be as prepared as possible throughout the year. The two entrances into Aries and a brief one into Pisces by Jupiter will all have a dramatic effect on you, mostly manifested as higher assertiveness and confidence. This might be just the fuel you need to get you over a few extra miles to finally finish any long-standing projects that you've had in progress. In general, 2022 might just be the year where many of your professional dreams will come true. Growth, self-discovery, and change will be common themes for Pisces folk this year. These important changes and the accompanying confusion can lead to some discomfort and anxiety, but there will be no cause to despair or give in to fear as the planets are in your favor.

Chapter 8: Physical and Mental Health

When it comes to health, nothing can beat the advice of a qualified medical professional, which the writer of this book certainly isn't. Your astrological outlook will be useful in predicting certain aspects and telling you what to look out for, and it's difficult to go wrong with prevention when it comes to looking after yourself. If you encounter health issues that pose an immediate risk or concern, however, astrology won't do you much good in the way of mending an existing problem. With that said, we'll take a look at what the planets might have in store when it comes to health, paying heed to any potential hints.

One health concern that can affect virtually everyone when a new year begins is stress. Thinking about all the goals we want to set and accomplish – and all the important endeavors that await us can become overwhelming and stressful. Things can go from bad to worse if the year gets underway and things get off to a seemingly bad start. This is why it's important to set realistic expectations and stay patient. Wellness is important every year, but with the potential for so many changes and novelties in 2022, this year might require even more care.

Aries

While Mars might be a bit shoddy at times this year, it will continue supplying Aries with as much of its inherent strength, fire, and intense energy as possible. Mercury's first retrograde in 2022 will affect you in regard to health, but the effect will actually be mostly positive. This retrograde will be a good time to work on any routines pertaining to your health and overall well-being. You might want to consider starting to exercise more regularly or begin a wellness program, particularly if you have a friend to accompany you.

Both Jupiter and Mercury will make transits and sign entrances that will affect areas of your life, including closure, coping, sacrifice, and therapy. In spring, make sure that you don't neglect your mental health. Physical exercise is always beneficial in that regard, but you also have to mind the stressors in your life and give yourself the relief you need when you need it. Early April will be a good time for you to hatch new plans and start anew, which makes this a good time to begin adopting some healthy regimens and habits for the long term. You should first do some introspective thinking to see which aspect of your health needs the most attention and then make plans accordingly.

Taurus

Since 2022 will put a strong emphasis on self-improvement for Taureans, your health and overall well-being should receive the majority of your attention. Venus' retrograde through Capricorn and its other movements will motivate you to spend some time thinking about how you're treating your health and how that might be improved. Even if you have an intricate daily routine that aims for wellness, maybe it's time to make some adjustments and changes with new ideas that could provide more benefit.

In May, Jupiter will initiate a season that favors outdoor activity for Taureans, so you might consider spending more time in nature from May 10 onward. It will also be a great time to try things like meditation, keeping a journal, and improving your sleep cycle, all of which can have immense benefits for your mental health. The entry of Venus into Leo in August has the potential to affect your emotional side of you, particularly as it relates to your familial relationships. In line with the theme of relaxation and taking it easy, your regular exercise could also be bolstered with indoor activity when you're not out and about.

Gemini

In 2022, it will be paramount for Geminis to pay more attention to their health and give themselves the care and attention that they need physically, mentally, and spiritually. The positioning and transits of the North and South Nodes will affect your level of mindfulness and your daily routines. In 2022, it'll be important for you to analyze your life, identify any influences that have a detrimental effect on your health in any way, and take steps to get rid of those influences.

Eclipses will be another important player in Gemini's health and well-being this year. Their influence will be highly positive and energizing. If you've been struggling to kick a bad habit, for instance, this astrological vigor will give you the push that you need to triumph over your weaknesses. Don't misinterpret that energy as an invitation to resign yourself to fate and hope for your problems to solve themselves. You'll still have to keep struggling to make these changes; only now you'll have help in that fight. Late October might bring a reduction in your overall energy because of Mars' retrograde, but you can take that as an opportunity to relax and mull over some other steps you can take toward becoming healthier when you feel up to it.

Cancer

The people-pleasing Cancer folks will do well to at least somewhat readjust their focus back on some of their own needs in 2022. There's nothing wrong with helping others and being someone others can lean on, of course, but when this comes at the expense of your well-being and interests on a regular basis, the consequences can be highly negative. Your mental health and emotional well-being can be particularly affected. Since you are at the risk of going down this road, you'll have to retake some control in the near future and reassess where your energy is going and how much of it you're getting back.

That give-take balance can be difficult to achieve when you're all about selflessness and compassion, but this will be a hill you have to climb. The time is nigh for you to introduce some novelties in your life, and what better way is there to do that other than through new hobbies, exercise routines, and wellness programs? Meditation can go a long way toward alleviating some of your accumulated stress, while an even better alternative would be a relaxing trip to some kind of distant retreat.

Leo

2022 will be a good year for Leos to set some significant health goals for themselves. Under the influence of Venus and Pluto, you have the potential to get started on this from very early in the year. With Venus in retrograde and Pluto positioned to affect Leo in all things health-related, it's a time to reflect and pay heed to your body and mind. If you've been working too hard or obsessing over other people's perceptions of you, it's only natural that you'll tire, as energetic and radiant as Leos might be. Take a long hard look at your life and well-being as 2022 goes underway and ask yourself if your work has worn you out and taken a toll on your mental health.

Jupiter's entrance into Pisces will give you a window of opportunity for healing and introspection, which you should use to address some sources of stress in your life. If you find yourself in need of emotional or any other kind of support, April will be a good time to rely on your friends and family. In general, 2022 will be the year in which you should change the way you live to accommodate your overall well-being better.

Virgo

By its nature, the sign of Virgo is one of health, well-being, and development in the mental, physical, and spiritual sense. Saturn will continue energizing you in this regard, helping you establish and maintain healthy daily routines while also blessing you with its organizational qualities. 2022 will be an excellent year to introduce even more healthy routines, as everything you do concerning health will produce great results.

However, the aspect between Uranus and Saturn in September and October will introduce some tension, which can lead to stress and indecisiveness. If you find yourself in these murky waters, it's best to keep focusing on your exercise and wellness routines, even going the extra mile to intensify them. Your astrological influences, combined with your physical efforts, can result in major positive transformations, both physical and mental, making 2022 a good year to work out and elevate training. Make sure you don't neglect your diet, *as a healthy, quality diet is half the battle when it comes to exercise.*

Libra

The retrograde of Libra's ruling Venus shifts the focus inward and cools things down. It's still going to be important to maintain a healthy lifestyle throughout January, but it's a good idea to try and somehow combine healthy living with the solitude and introspection that this retrograde will inspire in you. The perfect compromise would be to intensify your exercise and training at home. Maybe a good way to start 2022 would be to build a small home gym or at least purchase some exercise tools or machines for your home.

The influences of Venus and Pluto will work together well to keep you feeling good while also driving you to keep discipline and structure in your life, sticking with a healthy routine. Jupiter will likely bring you good health during its May transition through Pisces. It's a good idea to use this opportunity to make additional improvements, such as through your diet. Positive health trends will continue for you when the influences of Jupiter and Neptune start working together, especially if you maintain your good habits. The spring of 2022 will be a particularly good time to take a little vacation to rejuvenate and heal.

Scorpio

Scorpio's already secretive and withdrawn nature is likely to be exacerbated by the retrograde of Venus and the conjunction with Pluto in Capricorn, which might have some negative effects on your emotional and mental well-being if you become too withdrawn after New Year's. Another potential issue may arise if, in your effort to minimize social contact, you end up foregoing important doctor's appointments or check-ups. As such, early 2022 will be a time for you to try and strike a balance between your reclusive inclinations and your very real and objective need to maintain some contacts outside of just work.

This phase won't last long, though, and you should leave it with a better understanding of your priorities, particularly in your relationships. In your time of introspection and reflection, you might realize that some of your relationships don't bring you much beyond stress and frustration and that it might be time to cut them loose to conserve your emotional and mental strength. You'll feel greatly reinvigorated with the entrance of Mars into Capricorn and the combination of its influence with Venus. Your strength will return, and you'll feel energized to get into new routines.

Sagittarius

Uranus might bring quite a bit of disruption into the life of Sagittarians this year, and this influence will clash with Saturn to bring much confusion. Burdensome thoughts might accumulate to a point where they get mixed up and create a degree of chaos in your head. This won't necessarily be a long phase, though, especially if you put in the effort to initiate an overall reset to your routines and wellness, which are overdue in 2022. As part of that reset, it might be a good idea to try some new things like mindfulness, which might be just the thing you need to correlate some of those rogue thoughts.

Through its disruptions, Uranus will eventually help you see where the problems lie and what you can do to change things for the better. You'll eventually feel motivated to make changes and try alternatives. The entrance of the South Node into Scorpio will also help you identify some dead wood in your life, especially in regard to bad habits, which you'll be well advised to dispose of. Eclipses will shed even more light on the faults in your lifestyle, and by the end of the year, you should be well on your way toward meaningful improvements.

Capricorn

The influences of Venus and Pluto early in the year will set you up for some positive effects further down the line, but in the short term, you might run into some chop when it comes to your health. Of course, it's nothing to be alarmed about, especially if you stay focused on healthy living and fostering good habits, which shouldn't be too difficult for a Capricorn.

The retrograde of Venus will make you reflect on some things, including your health. You'll walk away from this retrograde with a better understanding of your own body, how you are treating it, and what it might need. Something else you'll likely realize during this time is that happiness and fulfillment are just as important to you this year as work, physical health, and anything else in life because that's what your mental well-being will depend on. This is why taking steps toward making yourself happier and more content will indirectly result in you working on your health. There will be even more opportunities to take a step back and rethink some of your habits as Mars begins its October retrograde. In the end, you'll find that slowing down is precisely what you need in your life.

Aquarius

For the Water Bearers out there, 2022 will be the year where ridding yourselves of stress is the name of the game. You might think that you haven't been stressed through 2021, and if that's the case, then you should use the ongoing retrograde of Venus to reexamine your lifestyle as objectively as possible. When you find that you've been stressing and putting your mental well-being low on your list of priorities, as many Aquarians will, you'll realize that 2022 is a time for changes. It might not just work that's pressuring you, though. Perhaps you've been neglecting your well-being for the sake of someone else, maybe even someone who really doesn't deserve it.

You have to break free from these shackles, mentally and spiritually recuperate, and then adopt a new, healthy routine if need be. In time, you'll find that these changes will have a positive effect not just on your health but also on your productivity and motivation. Beware that Saturn doesn't make you feel too constricted and trapped this year, and instead, use this planet's energies of structure and rules to help you become more disciplined and organized.

Pisces

This year, people under this sign will really have the planets working for their spiritual and emotional stability. The Jupiter-Neptune conjunction in Pisces on April 12 will have an important effect on your spirituality because of how it energizes your sign's already renowned intuition. As a consequence, you'll feel particularly in tune with your spiritual side, drawing all the serenity, wisdom, and strength you need right from the spiritual realm. This peace of mind will serve your mental health perfectly well.

You should also view these favorable conditions as an opportunity to get more involved in wellness, exercise, meditation, and other practices that might make you even more balanced. Mindfulness and yoga can also be highly beneficial to such an intuitive and reflective sign. Nonetheless, some Pisces will enter this year with residual issues and pains from before, but 2022 will be the year to address and resolve these things in a healthy, permanent manner. If such problems are related to certain people, then one of the best things you can do for your overall health is resolve those issues and turn a new leaf. July will be a particularly favorable month to start exercising and working out if that's the path you choose for this year.

Chapter 9: Wealth and Finance

As we briefly mentioned earlier, the ongoing Venus retrograde will affect business, which will inevitably spill over into finances as well. This will change after January, of course, so the overall outlook for 2022 in regard to finances is rather positive. Caution is advised, however, particularly in how you spend your money this year.

The four Mercury retrogrades in 2022 might make you more inclined to buy things impulsively, leading to regrets. As such, you should be careful not to rush into substantial purchases or, if you do, it's best to make sure you can take your money back if you change your mind. You can expect a considerable influx of cash by the end of July because of the aspect between Uranus and the North Node in Taurus.

The eclipses can also be expected to leave their mark on your finances. These eclipses are likely to reward those who save their money and spend it wisely. Jupiter will also substantially affect how we spend, landing us into episodes of impulsive spending and generous giving. In all, the year will bring many opportunities, and as long as you are careful how you spend your money, you should come out of 2022 richer than you entered it.

Aries

The bold Aries can look forward to quite a few victories this year, and those are likely to pay off monetarily. Despite the retrograde of Venus messing stuff up for many people, Aries can look forward to prosperity and abundance as early as January 18, owing to the North Node and its association with Taurus at that time. Assuming you've been responsible and have made some viable financial plans in the previous year, you are likely to start reaping the benefits by March 12. The solar and lunar eclipses of April 30 and November 8 will herald even more returns on all the efforts you'll have invested by that time. If you've been building a business for years up to this point, you can expect this year to bring a major payoff.

If you're anticipating or just hoping for a raise, this year will have good things in store for you. If you're not expecting an already discussed raise, this year will be a good time to bring up the subject with your employers because of the elevated likelihood of success. This means that despite the planets being inclined to assist you with a little push of fate, you might need to initiate things, depending on your situation.

Taurus

The fresh new opportunities that await Taurus in 2022 are likely to be quite lucrative. Your year should involve a lucrative start and end, with a prolonged period of prosperous stability in between. Under the influence of Saturn, the added income in 2022 should come as the result of a new job that will entail more responsibility and thus a better paycheck. Even when everyone else struggles to progress professionally and get recognition, Taureans should continue to prosper. February is likely to be particularly important in this regard, especially early in the month.

You can expect the greatest changes to come around the onset of winter. November brings a heightened creative drive into your life, which will then translate into professional developments and, eventually, monetary gains. It's possible that promotion around this time might even land you in a position of authority over other people, depending on your job, which will entail a lot of responsibility and due rewards. Some Taureans might even end up in the public limelight as a result of these successes, assuming their job or business venture entail such possibilities. In all, you can expect at least several financial opportunities this year, but beware that you don't get blinded by the dollar bills to the point where you forget other aspects of your work, such as fulfillment and pleasure.

Gemini

Geminis will also have all manner of creative forces working in their favor this year, leading to the birth of many ideas that could bring about great new opportunities. Let your creativity flow even when thinking about ways of making money, and you might be surprised by the paths that suddenly open up to you. Thanks to astrological influences bolstering ambition and drive, you'll have the means to make these ideas a reality in 2022. It's a great year for expression all around, so don't hesitate to follow your passions. As long as you follow them, you'll likely land in situations that will bring some substantial bucks your way.

With that said, you would certainly be wise to exercise due caution before making decisive moves, especially if such moves involve reallocating your money and investing it. Passion is one thing, but uninformed, reckless spending won't get you very far. When it comes to investments, 2022 will be a good year for buying properties, which will prove far less risky than various schemes that may or may not work out in your favor. As for long-term ideas that you've been mulling over for a while, autumn will be the best time to put your plans into action.

Cancer

2022 will bring luck to Cancers when it comes to their own money, but existing financial relations are likely to be somewhat infringed upon by Saturn, affecting your opportunities to secure loans, for instance. That said, May 10 heralds the beginning of a season that brings opportunities in which your efforts will be recognized and rewarded thanks to Jupiter's entrance into the area of the chart associated with careers. All this means is that you'll be unlikely to be given or lent money but will have more than enough luck when it comes to making money through your work.

It will also be a good idea to reorganize your eggs into a few more baskets, diversifying your income as much as possible. If time allows, you should seize new opportunities that might bring financial gains on the side, in addition to your main occupation. The stars will hold entrepreneurial Cancers in favor, blessing new ventures and ideas as you present them to the world. March, April, and October will be particularly lucky months in regard to launching something new. All these opportunities and endeavors will elevate your risk of overworking yourself, though, so it's going to be important to take care of yourself and give yourself a treat now and then.

Leo

For Leos, 2022 has the potential to bring a bit of uncertainty and unpredictability. As negative as that might sound at first glance, the truth is that unpredictability works both ways when it comes to money and in no way means that you'll have a bad year. You'll shift some of your focus on personal growth and happiness, trying to get more fulfillment out of your work, and in doing so, the chances are good that you'll reach for a promotion or new position. Such advancements are likely to bring monetary gain, but for many Leos, the real prize will be a greater sense of satisfaction and accomplishment as they land into a position where they feel most comfortable.

This year, a change of careers is possible for many Leos, largely owing to the uncertainty that Uranus brings into the mix. This will also be a good year for Leos to focus on fiscal consolidation and control, so you should ensure you have a strong grip on your expenses. Whenever you find yourself making a significant purchase this year, it'll be a good idea to ask yourself twice if you really need it.

Virgo

Virgos might have quite an exciting year in 2022 regarding their finances, especially if they make good use of their networks. It will also be a good year for promoting yourself, your skills, and your work, an endeavor where a network of people will be particularly useful. Every business contact will count in 2022, and if you make good use of them, you can expect big payoffs in the second half of the year.

Virgos will potentially overwork themselves this year, especially in service of others earlier during the year. You must make sure not to forego your own needs and well-being, regardless of how eager you are to work hard. You can also expect some pretty significant developments if you continuously put in the effort to enact your novel ideas. These ideas can bring substantial financial gains as the year progresses, so you just need to remember to keep working but not work too hard and exercise some patience. Your due is bound to come after a while, even if the year starts off a bit slow.

Libra

Libras can look forward to quite a bit of luck in their finances in 2022, which somewhat ironically also spawns a need for caution. Libras who show initiative and chart new professional grounds on their own will be rewarded, but with a lot of luck come many opportunities to mess up. If you are interested in living a self-employment life, 2022 might just be the year when you make it happen. It will also be a good year for you to work on various personal projects or try your hand at consulting.

Many of these ventures can result in financial uncertainty and instability for a while, so be prepared for that. Securing some excess finances before embarking on a new venture into the unknown would certainly mitigate some of the risks. If possible, however, it's best to make the shift into self-employment gradual by working on the side and holding onto your main occupation for as long as it takes to get your business idea off the ground. It might require very hard work for a while, but it's certainly a goal worth pursuing in 2022. Take breaks wherever you can and catch a breather while also keeping your financial situation under wraps, as there might be quite a few wandering eyes this year.

Scorpio

2022 brings immense financial potential for Scorpios, especially in the second half of the year. An improvement in your finances this year will be an opportunity that you might want to use to pay off or reduce some of your debts if such exist. Thanks to the plentiful opportunities to make money this year, it's the best time to unburden yourself, avoid incurring new debts – *and be done with this issue once and for all.*

In April, May, and December, conditions will be favorable for Scorpios to make deals and investments, but it's important not to rush into the unknown. Given the sheer number of opportunities expected to come your way this year, it can be easy to get carried away and lost in the proverbial woods. You might also find 2022 to be a year of major transitions as one of those new opportunities turns into a whole new job and career path. Things might slow down a bit in the second half of the year if you are involved in purchasing and selling properties, but these will mostly be temporary delays.

Sagittarius

Archers who have hobbies in which they invest a lot of time, care, and enjoyment will be happy to hear that 2022 might bring an opportunity for them to capitalize on those hobbies big time. The most important thing for Sagittarius folks in these endeavors will be consistency and a proactive approach. This means that if you want to turn your hobby into a source of income, for instance, you'll have to take concrete steps to make that happen and then continue taking all the additional steps required. In essence, when you get on the move, that's when you'll start seeing just how inclined the stars are toward you this year.

Your best bet is to stay on your own and avoid partnerships this year. Focus on one project at a time, stay patient, and you'll find that February, June, and November will be particularly favorable. All the hard work you put in this year will pay off many times over in due time, while the planets will continue inspiring one novel idea after another in your mind. Another thing to beware of is excess spending, as 2022 won't be a good year for Archers who like to throw money around.

Capricorn

Capricorns are likely to get off to a slow start in 2022, but the middle of the year should bring a wave of opportunities, especially for well-informed investments. As such, the first half of the year will be well-spent in research, planning, and risk calculation to make sure that your eventual investments will have as strong of a base as possible. Simply put, the best kinds of investments for Capricorns in 2022 will be conservative, careful ones.

The situation will be similar for Capricorns searching for a job, whether to get out of unemployment or change their job. Halfway into June is roughly the time when prospects for employment should improve dramatically. This gives you plenty of time in early 2022 to consider your options, think about your career path, figure out where you want to go, or just spend time picking up new skills. This year will put Capricorns at some risk of burnout as some of you might get a bit too obsessed with your work, which will require moderation if you are to avoid your work taking over every aspect of your life.

Aquarius

Aquarius is another sign that can expect some uncertainties and unexpected twists and turns in 2022's finances. This year's eclipses will have ramifications for Aquarians, and their finances mostly manifested as randomness and instability. It's a good time to reevaluate some of your long-term plans and make the necessary adjustments if unexpected opportunities or problems crop up.

Aquarians will stay very busy this year, undoubtedly bringing a fair share of financial benefits that tend to accompany hard work. The randomness of 2022 can be a stimulating experience, and somewhere in those twists and turns, you might become aware of options that you didn't even know existed. This year will also bring a certain degree of luck for Aquarians who engage in speculation, so a speculative financial venture or two on the side might pay off big time. Just make sure you don't gamble anything you aren't willing to lose. Aquarians will also benefit from other types of investments and self-promotion in 2022, especially in February, April, and October. If you're trying to get a product or service out there, these months might be the perfect time for a new advertising campaign.

Pisces

Pisces people will benefit greatly from their creativity this year. The creative ideas you get in 2022 will enrich your life and make your existence much more fulfilling. These ideas will also provide you with financial benefits to reap in due time. However, in the grand scheme, Pisces can expect their finances to be a bit fickle and variable in 2022. This instability probably won't incur major losses or anything, but it will probably require some improvisation and brainstorming on your part, which, in turn, will bolster your creativity even further.

In the end, potential challenges might easily turn into financial victories. Pisces will likely see solid returns if they exercise a bit more boldness and are willing to give new things a try. Episodes of substantial financial gain will alternate with periods of uncertainty. When the latter strikes, you can take comfort in the knowledge that a better situation will be following shortly thereafter. It's also a good idea for Pisces to consider investing if they have disposable income, particularly in April, June, and July. You might also benefit greatly from studying a subject or skill set that interests you, which could open up opportunities for a career change down the line.

Chapter 10: Life-Changing Resolutions

Whether you're a fan of making New Year's resolutions or not, you might want to consider making one or two now that you've been thoroughly acquainted with what astrology has in store for your 2022. This information can help you develop some of your own resolutions or adjust a resolution you've already been thinking about to accommodate the horoscope you've just read and increase the odds of following through on your promises. To make things even easier for you, we'll take one last chapter to go over the twelve zodiac signs and a few recommended resolutions that might have the best potential to come to fruition, based on your astrological readings.

Remember that 2022 is mostly a year of changes and novelties, which can make or break a year when it comes to resolutions. This will depend on the kind of resolution you make and how much effort you put into following through, but new energies can give you the strength that you need to stay true to your word. Similarly, the changes can lead to a few unexpected outcomes that could potentially disrupt even the best-laid plans. However, knowing your astrological forecast makes such eventualities less likely to surprise you.

Aries

For Aries, 2022 will be a year to get active and adopt healthy habits and routines, particularly in the physical sense. To that end, one resolution you might want to try is to begin meditating. At first glance, Aries's character is the opposite of tranquility and meditation, but that's precisely the point. Your fiery sign's chaotic ways might be perfectly countered by meditation. Meditation will help you get a grip on yourself in a way that ensures you'll dissipate less of your energy around on pointless things.

The energy reserves that Aries carriers around might simply become too much to bear this year. Meditation will help you stay in control, but if you want to truly expend that excess energy, you'll want to get physically active, which can be a second New Year's resolution for you. Adopt a training regimen, hire a professional, or simply start going to the gym on your own. Better yet, you can get involved in some kind of sports activity, which can provide mental stimulation while also involving a fairly holistic workout. Swimming, for instance, is one of the best physical activities to adopt.

Taurus

If you're a Taurus, you might find that the image you project to the world will be quite important for your state of mind in 2022. While you certainly shouldn't depend on the approval of others, projecting an image that makes you feel comfortable in the world can certainly bring a degree of fulfillment. In that regard, you should ask yourself how you're being perceived and what you want to change on that front. This can mean adopting a new clothing style or changing your appearance in another way. Whatever change you introduce might be just the refreshment you need to feel fresher in 2022.

Getting enough rest will be another important theme for you this year, which is why it should make its way into at least one of your New Year's resolutions. You might be inclined to think that only concrete accomplishments can be goals, but in reality, getting more rest and relaxing can be life goals that are just as important. If you've been overworking yourself, 2022 will be the perfect time to make a promise to your mind, body, and spirit that you'll take it easy and take a few steps back in 2022, letting yourself recuperate and recharge the batteries when need be.

Gemini

A great way to enrich your life and attain a profound sense of purpose in 2022 would be to satisfy your innate Gemini need to make a positive difference in the world. During the most laid-back month of January, it'll be a good time to mull over a few ideas of how you can help change the world, pick a cause, and commit yourself to it for this year. Activism and volunteering will be excellent ways to productively streamline some of your excess energy that could otherwise end up wasted or even misused for negative outcomes. A great way to stick to a resolution would be to involve a friend so that the two of you or an entire team can support and lean on each other to keep the cause going throughout the year.

An excellent and productive activity that can keep you occupied while allowing you to make a difference would be starting a podcast. If you're one of those Geminis known for enjoying conversation and public speaking, podcasts might be the perfect medium for you. It's also a very accessible hobby that virtually everyone can start with minimal equipment.

Cancer

As many Cancers thoroughly enjoy studying people, 2022 might be a good year to turn that interest inward. A great new hobby could emerge from the idea of studying yourself or, more precisely, your background, family history, and roots. Whether you decide to create a detailed, far-reaching family tree or just collect a bunch of stories of your ancestors, this kind of activity can give you plenty to do in your spare time. It can start with something as simple as talking to your dad or, better yet, grandparents and writing down a few names. Making a resolution about doing these things would be all about self-exploration and grounding. Apart from a new sense of perspective, you might also get closer to your family in the process.

Similarly, you might find it fulfilling to keep a daily journal in 2022, especially if you've never kept one before. You might find that it's an excellent way to channel your feelings and understand them better. Some things within us are much easier to understand when they are put on paper and made available for objective analysis.

Leo

For Leos, it could be beneficial to thoroughly reevaluate your career path, goals, and sources of fulfillment in life. Your resolution can simply be to introduce more self-care into your daily life or to change the way you work, but the important thing will be to make some promises to yourself to improve your professional life and make your work more satisfying.

The outgoing, radiant Leo is all about exerting influence and leaving a mark in the world, which is why you should consider volunteering in 2022. There are so many things to be passionate about when you care about the outside world and other people, and volunteering is probably the single best way to make your presence known, draw fulfillment from meaningful work, and simply help other people. You can also help animals by volunteering at a shelter or rescue service. Just a couple of days each month can immeasurably enrich the year ahead of you. You don't have to make your volunteering activities the focal point of your life or be out there in the streets every day to make a tangible difference. There are so many opportunities to do good in the world that even the smallest bit of help can be the most valuable contribution.

Virgo

A good way for Virgos to start the new year would be with a promise that you'll spend more time celebrating yourself and your accomplishments after all the hard work you've been putting in. This will help you shake those unpleasant feelings and sneaking suspicion that you're just not doing enough. Take the time to actually think objectively about every bit of effort you put in. You'll find that it adds up pretty fast and gives you a rather satisfactory summary of everything you've gotten done. Mindfulness can go a long way toward helping you be more present and aware of your effects in the world.

Virgos will be affected by 2022's expansion, growth, and transformation themes. To that end, it could be a very good idea to set some goals that will inspire similar changes in yourself. Maybe it's time to consider going back to school, attending a course or just picking up a few new skills on your own by learning on the internet. You can also simply opt to read more books in 2022, which will have the unavoidable consequence of expanding your mind.

Libra

Because of your inherent love of socialization, conversation, reading, and writing, you and many other Libras might find 2022 to be as good of a year as any to start learning a new language. Learning a language is always one of the best, most beneficial hobbies you can pick up, not to mention a straightforward New Year's resolution to set for yourself. However, as straightforward as it is, learning a new language can also be one of the more difficult resolutions to keep. A good way to stay the course and persevere is to tie the learning to a goal other than mastering the language in question. Wanting to take a trip to a certain country or living in a foreign culture for a while, for example, can be great motivators to keep studying.

Because so many Libras tend to be hyper-social, a resolution that's often relevant to their lives is to spend more time alone. This resolution works well in combination with other resolutions, which might require you to work on your own. The important thing is to give yourself some time to indulge in the activities you enjoy for your own sake and to spend some time in reflection instead of using every bit of your energy on everyone else.

Scorpio

On the opposite side of the spectrum, the withdrawn, private Scorpio is prone to spending too little time with others. A resolution relevant for many Scorpios each year is to decide to spend more time out and about. This can be a call to socialize more and mingle with others, but it's also possible to get out more without necessarily increasing your socialization too much. You can decide to spend more time in nature, for instance, going hiking, mountain climbing, hunting, or just taking your dog out to the great outdoors. Involving them in activities might be even better if you have a small yet close circle of valuable friends. Either way, all that matters is that you get out more and live a life that's a bit more active and stimulating.

Grudges and forgiveness are also common themes in the lives of Scorpio, and just like every year before 2022, you are invited to consider burying the war ax in outstanding conflicts and making amends with people. It will be easier to do this when you realize that you will be doing it for yourself. The key is to unburden yourself from this baggage that you carry around so you can make room for better, more productive things than holding a grudge.

Sagittarius

For Sagittarians, it's always a good idea to improve your art of saying "no" to people. With a propensity to get carried away, agree to way too many things, and go completely bonkers, wasting valuable energy on a million things at once, Archers should try and exert more control this year. The easiest way to start this is by paying more attention to your schedule and saying no to activities and people when you're overbooked.

As a sign of learning, growth, and adventure, any year is a good year for Sagittarians to start attending a new course, get into a school, or just adopt a new hobby that allows for mastery of a particular skill. You can spend time learning about things just to satisfy your curiosity, but practical knowledge can always have far-reaching consequences beyond just your short-term enjoyment and preoccupation. To stay the course, however, it's important to pick the right topic or area of study and make it as specific as you can. Broad topics with plenty of unexpected turns have a way of tiring you out faster, which spells an untimely end for your New Year's resolution.

Capricorn

On the broader side of things, the driven, ambitious, and hard-working Capricorn will always do well to take a few steps back and spend some time in self-care. Make a promise to yourself that you'll not lose sight of your own needs just so you can chase ten projects simultaneously. By all means, keep working hard, but try to make this year all about your personal fulfillment, health, and as much leisure as possible.

Because 2022 will be a good year for Capricorns to start on a new career path, a New Year's resolution to that end might come in handy. Utilize your inherent nature and character to make quality plans that reach a considerable way into the future. By sitting down for one whole day and brainstorming the many ways in which you can change and improve your professional path, you'll be able to come up with something like a five-year plan. Because of your sign's inherent discipline and perseverance, sticking to that plan should be easier than it would be for other signs, but it's still a good idea to make your plans as specific and detailed as possible.

Aquarius

The Water Bearer's tendency to get carried away in your creative world of ideas, projects, and studies often result in reduced social contact. As you well know, it's not that the Aquarian lacks social skills, but you simply don't hesitate to put people as a second or even third priority once you get immersed in your work. If that's been the case with you recently, then a good New Year would resolve to reconnect with all friends and rejuvenate important relationships that might have gone a bit cold. As always, you should focus on quality over quantity, only committing yourself to those relationships that were positive and fulfilling in the past. If a relationship ended or went cold for some concrete reason, then you should ask yourself if that reason was good enough before reestablishing contact.

A great way to restart an old friend would be to invite your old pal on a trip somewhere special. This year might be a good one for budget travel to save money and stimulate your problem-solving mind with the organization of such a trip.

Pisces

As we briefly mentioned earlier in the book, the intuitive and reflective Pisces will have ample opportunity for spirituality in 2022. Whatever you think might suit your specific needs to improve your spirituality will be an activity worth pursuing. Yoga, meditation, going back to church, reading ancient texts, or getting involved in certain groups can all be valuable resolutions in this regard. The important thing is to balance yourself and drown out some of the static that might have accumulated in your mind and soul over the last couple of years.

Of course, the act of helping, in itself, is often a spiritual experience, so you too should consider volunteering for certain causes. Abandoned animals, children, the homeless, and many other folks and creatures down on their luck are out there in the thousands, needing all the help they can get. Whatever city and country you find yourself in, the chances are good that there are ample opportunities to volunteer and be a humanitarian, at least in your spare time.

Conclusion

No matter how inclined the stars might be toward being on your side, astrological odds and predictions can still never be substitutes for things like hard work, good judgment, and carefulness. You can use what the stars are telling you to know what you might expect or to inspire hope, but what you don't want to do is rely on them to take charge of your life and solve your problems. Even when you have the perfect astrological outlook, it's important to be prepared for the worst. As humans, we are blessed and cursed with free will, allowing us a fair degree of freedom and the ability to make bad decisions and get in trouble no matter how much the odds might be in our favor.

In all, 2022 has the potential to be a very good year for you, but you have to remember that good fortune will only take you so far. Astrology is all about letting you know when opportunities will arise for you to act to your benefit. It's going to be up to you to recognize these opportunities in your life and do what it takes to seize them and make them work for you.

Your astrological outlook should also hopefully help you see what changes you can introduce into your life at the start of the year. As opposed to making resolutions on a whim or in the heat of the moment, the forecasts in this book have hopefully given you something to base your new year's resolutions on. Many resolutions fail because of unexpected factors that show up throughout the year, but when you know what to expect beforehand, the foundations of your resolutions should be stronger. The important thing is to know that there is a lot to look forward to, even when the going gets tough.

Here's another book by Mari Silva that you might like

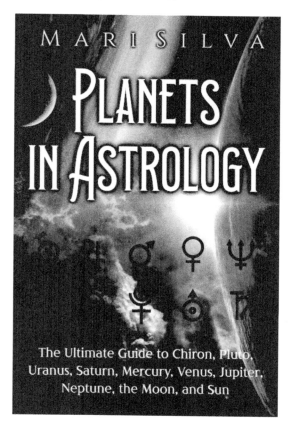

Your Free Gift (only available for a limited time)

Thanks for getting this book! If you want to learn more about various spirituality topics, then join Mari Silva's community and get a free guided meditation MP3 for awakening your third eye. This guided meditation mp3 is designed to open and strengthen ones third eye so you can experience a higher state of consciousness. Simply visit the link below the image to get started.

https://spiritualityspot.com/meditation

Resources

2022 Horoscopes. (n.d.). Www.horoscope.com. from
https://www.horoscope.com/us/horoscopes/yearly/2022-horoscope-overview.aspx

2022 Planetary Overview | Cafe Astrology .com. (n.d.).
Cafeastrology.com. Retrieved from
https://cafeastrology.com/astrology-of-2022.html#calendar

A Beginner's Guide To The 12 Houses Of The Horoscope. (2020,
August 31). Mindbodygreen.
https://www.mindbodygreen.com/articles/the-12-houses-of-astrology

April 2, 2020, & Stapleton, D. (n.d.). Aries Zodiac Sign:
Characteristics, Dates, & More.
Www.astrology.com. https://www.astrology.com/zodiac-signs/aries

April 6, 2020, & Stapleton, D. (n.d.). Leo Zodiac Sign: Characteristics,
Dates, & More.
Www.astrology.com. https://www.astrology.com/zodiac-signs/leo

Archive, V. A., & feed, G. author R. (2021, November 16). What is a
birth chart in astrology —

and how do you read one? New York Post. https://nypost.com/article/astrology-birth-chart

Aries Horoscope: Aries Zodiac Sign Dates Compatibility, Traits and Characteristics. (2019).

Astrology-Zodiac-Signs.com. https://www.astrology-zodiac-signs.com/zodiac-signs/aries

Astrology.com. (n.d.). 2022 Astrology Predictions: The Tide is Turning | Astrology.com.

Www.astrology.com. Retrieved from

https://www.astrology.com/article/2022-astrology-predictions

Australis, V. (2021, December 31). Your Love Horoscope For 2022 Is Here, & These Are The Dates When Luck Is On Your Side. Www.refinery29.com. https://www.refinery29.com/en-us/2021/12/10711916/love-horoscope-2022

Backlund, R. (2021, December 16). Let 2021 Go! Your 2022 Horoscope Predicts a Very

Different Year. StyleCaster. https://stylecaster.com/2022-horoscopes

Booth, P. (2021, December 23). Your special 2022 horoscope: Prepare for a year of progress.

CBC.

https://www.cbc.ca/life/culture/your-special-2022-horoscope-prepare-for-a-year-of-progress-1.6293938

Campbell, S. (2021, December 7). The New Year's Resolutions Each Zodiac Sign Needs to

Survive 2022. StyleCaster. https://stylecaster.com/zodiac-sign-new-years-resolutions/#slide-2

Cancer Horoscope: Cancer Zodiac Sign Dates Compatibility, Traits, and Characteristics. (2019a). Astrology-Zodiac-Signs.com.

https://www.astrology-zodiac-signs.com/zodiac-signs/cancer

Cancer Horoscope: Cancer Zodiac Sign Dates Compatibility, Traits, and Characteristics.

(2019b). Astrology-Zodiac-Signs.com.

https://www.astrology-zodiac-signs.com/zodiac-signs/cancer

Capricorn Horoscope: Capricorn Zodiac Sign Dates Compatibility, Traits and Characteristics.

(2020). Astrology-Zodiac-Signs.com.

https://www.astrology-zodiac-signs.com/zodiac-signs/capricorn

Chinese horoscope 2022 - Year of Tiger, 12 Animals Forecast. (2021, December 29).

KarmaWeather.

https://www.karmaweather.com/news/yearly-chinese-horoscope/predictions-2022

Dec 20, L. S. (2021, December 20). Your 2022 Sex and Love Horoscope. InStyle. https://www.instyle.com/lifestyle/astrology/sex-love-horoscope-2022

Faragher, A. K. (2018, March 12). An Astrology Beginner's Guide to Reading Your Own Birth Chart. Allure. https://www.allure.com/story/astrology-birth-chart-reading

Faragher, A. K. (2021, June 3). What Your Moon Sign Reveals About Your Emotional Personality. Allure. https://www.allure.com/story/zodiac-moon-sign-emotional-personality

February 29, 2020, & Stapleton, D. (n.d.). Capricorn Zodiac Sign: Characteristics, Dates, & More. Www.astrology.com. https://www.astrology.com/zodiac-signs/capricorn

Freed, J. (2021, December 30). An Astrological Forecast for 2022. Goop.

https://goop.com/wellness/spirituality/horoscope-predictions-2022

Gemini Horoscope: Gemini Zodiac Sign Dates Compatibility, Traits, and Characteristics. (2019). Astrology-Zodiac-Signs.com. https://www.astrology-zodiac-signs.com/zodiac-signs/gemini

Horoscope career 2022. (2022, January 1). Vogue India. https://www.vogue.in/horoscope/collection/horoscope-career-2022

How to interpret your Birth Chart. (n.d.). Tree of Life. https://treeoflife.com.au/blogs/news/how-to-interpret-your-birth-chart

Hunt, A. (2022, January 9). Love horoscope 2022: What relationships and romances are in store

for your star sign this year? Woman and Home Magazine. https://www.womanandhome.com/life/love-horoscope-2022

Jiang, F. (2022, January 4). Year of the Tiger (2022, 2010, 1998, 1986, 1974) : Luck &

Personality. China Highlights. https://www.chinahighlights.com/travelguide/chinese-zodiac/tiger.htm

King, K. (2021, December 30). All the key astrological events of 2022 to add to your calendar.

Metro. https://metro.co.uk/2021/12/30/astrology-all-the-key-events-of-2022-to-add-to-your-calendar-15836349

Leo Horoscope: Leo Zodiac Sign Dates Compatibility, Traits and Characteristics. (2000). Astrology-Zodiac-Signs.com. https://www.astrology-zodiac-signs.com/zodiac-signs/leo

Libra Horoscope: Zodiac Sign Dates Compatibility, Traits, and Characteristics. (2019). Astrology-Zodiac-Signs.com. https://www.astrology-zodiac-signs.com/zodiac-signs/libra

Love Horoscope 2022. (2022, January 2). Vogue India.

https://www.vogue.in/horoscope/collection/love-horoscope-2022

Luppino, O. (2021, December 21). Aries (March 20-April 19): Take Up Meditation.

POPSUGAR Smart Living.

https://www.popsugar.com/smart-living/photo-gallery/48644805/image/48659373/Aries-March-20-April-19-Take-Up-Meditation

Marriage Horoscope 2022: Tie the Knot, the Right Way. (n.d.). GaneshaSpeaks. Retrieved from https://www.ganeshaspeaks.com/2022-horoscope/marriage-horoscope-2022

Mesa, V. (2021, December 27). What Does Wellness Mean For You in 2022? Here's What Your Horoscope Says. POPSUGAR Smart Living. https://www.popsugar.com/smart-living/health-wellness-horoscope-2022-48652385

Monthly Horoscopes 2022-2023 For Each Zodiac Sign. (n.d.). Sun Signs. Retrieved from https://www.sunsigns.org/monthly-horoscope

Nast, C. (2021, December 23). Your Sign's 2022 Horoscope Predictions Are Here. Allure. https://www.allure.com/story/2022-horoscope-yearly-predictions

Pisces Horoscope: Pisces Zodiac Sign Dates Compatibility, Traits and Characteristics. (2019). Astrology-Zodiac-Signs.com. https://www.astrology-zodiac-signs.com/zodiac-signs/pisces

published, A. H. (2021, December 31). Your 2022 money horoscope revealed: What to expect from your finances and career in the year ahead. Woman and Home Magazine. https://www.womanandhome.com/life/money-horoscope/Scorpio

Horoscope: Scorpio Zodiac Sign Dates Compatibility, Traits, and Characteristics.

(2020). Astrology-Zodiac-Signs.com.

https://www.astrology-zodiac-signs.com/zodiac-signs/scorpio

Simone, E. (2021, December 29). Here's How to Find Your Rising Sign in Astrology. Allure. https://www.allure.com/story/rising-sign-personality-traits-astrology-ascendant-signs

Stapleton, D. (n.d.-a). Aquarius Zodiac Sign: Characteristics, Dates, & More | Astrology.com.

Www.astrology.com. https://www.astrology.com/zodiac-signs/aquarius

Stapleton, D. (n.d.-b). Cancer Zodiac Sign: Characteristics, Dates, & More | Astrology.com.

Www.astrology.com. https://www.astrology.com/zodiac-signs/cancer

Stapleton, D. (n.d.-c). Gemini Zodiac Sign: Characteristics, Dates, & More | Astrology.com.

Www.astrology.com. https://www.astrology.com/zodiac-signs/gemini

Stapleton, D. (n.d.-d). Libra Zodiac Sign: Characteristics, Dates, & More | Astrology.com.

Www.astrology.com. Retrieved from https://www.astrology.com/zodiac-signs/libra

Stapleton, D. (n.d.-e). Pisces Zodiac Sign: Characteristics, Dates, & More | Astrology.com.

Www.astrology.com. https://www.astrology.com/zodiac-signs/pisces

Stapleton, D. (n.d.-f). Sagittarius Zodiac Sign: Characteristics, Dates, & More | Astrology.com.

Www.astrology.com. https://www.astrology.com/zodiac-signs/sagittarius

Stapleton, D. (n.d.-g). Scorpio Zodiac Sign: Characteristics, Dates, & More | Astrology.com.

Www.astrology.com. https://www.astrology.com/zodiac-signs/scorpio

Stapleton, D. (n.d.-h). Taurus Zodiac Sign: Characteristics, Dates, & More | Astrology.com.

Www.astrology.com. https://www.astrology.com/zodiac-signs/taurus

Stapleton, D. (n.d.-i). Virgo Zodiac Sign: Characteristics, Dates, & More | Astrology.com.

Www.astrology.com. https://www.astrology.com/zodiac-signs/virgo

Stardust, L. (2022a, January 4). Your 2022 Career Horoscope Is Here, & These Dates Are

Bringing You Success. Www.refinery29.com. https://www.refinery29.com/en-us/2022/01/10711920/career-horoscope-2022

Stardust, L. (2022b, January 6). Your 2022 Money Horoscope Is Here, & These Dates May

Make Or Break Your Budget. Www.refinery29.com. https://www.refinery29.com/en-us/2022/01/10711918/money-horoscope-2022

Taurus Horoscope: Taurus Zodiac Sign Dates Compatibility, Traits and Characteristics. (2019).

Astrology-Zodiac-Signs.com. https://www.astrology-zodiac-signs.com/zodiac-signs/taurus

The 12 Houses in Astrology. (n.d.). Www.astrology-Zodiac-Signs.com. Retrieved from https://www.astrology-zodiac-signs.com/astrology/houses

The 12 Houses of the Horoscope Wheel. (2016). Astrostyle: Astrology and Daily, Weekly, Monthly Horoscopes by the AstroTwins. https://astrostyle.com/learn-astrology/the-12-zodiac-houses

The Houses in Astrology and Their Meaning | Astrology.com. (n.d.). Www.astrology.com.

Retrieved from https://www.astrology.com/houses

The North Nodes & South Node: Past Life Astrology. (n.d.). Astrostyle: Astrology and Daily, Weekly, Monthly Horoscopes by the AstroTwins. https://astrostyle.com/learn-astrology/north-south-nodes

The Planets in Astrology and Their Meaning | Astrology.com. (n.d.). Www.astrology.com.

Retrieved from https://www.astrology.com/planets

Valente, D. (2021, December 10). Important astrology events in 2022 that are worthy of your

attention. My Imperfect Life. https://www.myimperfectlife.com/features/astrology-events-in-2022

Virgo Horoscope: Virgo Zodiac Sign Dates Compatibility, Traits, and Characteristics. (2019).

Astrology-Zodiac-Signs.com. https://www.astrology-zodiac-signs.com/zodiac-signs/virgo

Ward, K. (2021, December 29). Your New Year's Resolution, by Zodiac Sign (and How to Keep

It). Cosmopolitan.